# BUCKEYES FOR LIFE

*Mark & Sarah,
You are Great Buckeyes!*

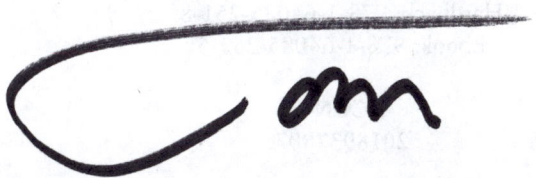

## TOM LEVENICK

Copyright © 2018 by Tom Levenick

All rights reserved. No part of this publication may be reproduced, distributed, or transmitted in any form or by any means, including photocopying, recording, or other electronic or mechanical methods, without the prior written permission of the publisher, except in the case of brief quotations embodied in critical reviews and certain other noncommercial uses permitted by copyright law. For permission requests, write to the publisher, addressed "Attention: Permissions Coordinator," at the address below.

Buckeyes for Life ltd
2172 Legends Dr.
Grove City, OH 43123
tom@buckeyesforlifebook.com

**IBSN #s**
Paperback: 978-1-64085-250-1
Hardback: 978-1-64085-251-8
Ebook: 978-1-64085-252-5

LCCN#
2018937807

# FOREWORD

"Ohio State Football is something very, very special.

It's not just on the field, where we have won eight National Championships and 36 Big Ten Championships, but it begins within our program where we recruit the finest athletes, who possess terrific character, integrity and family values. These characteristics, paired with the experience of sharing blood sweat, tears, broken bones and yes, championships, creates a "Buckeye Brotherhood" that is spiritual, life lasting and second to none. Those facts when combined with an incredible fan base, create one of the most incredible programs in college athletics.

Trust is one of the non-negotiable, critical elements of elite performance of any team. The highest levels of performance require the deepest levels of trust. When you have that trust, you get your best performance. Ohio State develops a loyal trust between players and coaches that lasts a lifetime.

At Ohio State, they develop the best players on the best team in college football, but they also work to develop young men into the best citizens that they can be in life after football. I am very proud that the Associated press recently named Ohio State the greatest college football program of all time, but I am even more proud that USA Today recently named Ohio State as the number one school in the nation for football and education. That is a major reason why the moms and dads of recruits from all over the country want their sons to play for the Scarlet and Gray. We have a "Buckeye Brotherhood and we are "Buckeyes for Life".

## Cornelius Green

- Ohio State Football 1972 – 1975
- Rose Bowl MVP – 1974
- Big Ten Most Valuable Player (1975)
- 2× First-team All-Big Ten (1974-1975)
- All-American 1975
- Hula Bowl MVP – 1976
- Ohio State Athletics Hall of Fame 1998

# CONTENTS

**Foreword**........................................... iii
**About the Author** ............................... vii
**Praises for Buckeyes for Life**.................... ix
**Dedication** ....................................... xi
**Acknowledgements**............................. xiii
**Introduction**.................................... xv

**Chapter One:** "You Win with People" ................. 1
**Chapter Two:** "Recruiting the Buckeye Way" ........... 9
**Chapter Three:** "Paying Forward" ................... 26
**Chapter Four:** Education and Development............ 45
**Chapter Five:** 'WE Remember Woody" ............... 57
**Chapter Six:** "The Buckeye Dynasty" ................. 72
- The People, The Tradition, The Excellence, The Pride & Passion

**Chapter Seven:** "The Rivalry" ...................... 82
**Chapter Eight:** "The Best Damn Band in the Land" .... 108
**Chapter Nine:** "Most Memorable Buckeye Experiences"... 123
- Former Players tell their stories: Rex Kern, Archie Griffin, Eddie George, John Brockington, Paul Warfield, Randy Gradishar, Chris Spielman, Joey Bosa, Ezekiel Elliott, Doug Plank, Ray Ellis, Eric Kumerow, Chris Carter, Tom Skladany, Jack Nicklaus, Lebron James and more.........

**Chapter Ten:** "What About Bob?" . . . . . . . . . . . . . . . . . 165
- Who was that one person in their life, that went out of their way to help develop and ensure future success for Former Buckeye Football Players?

**Chapter Eleven:** "Buckeyes for Life". . . . . . . . . . . . . . . . . 174
- Why is the Bond of Former Ohio State Football Players the strongest in College Football?

**Epilogue** . . . . . . . . . . . . . . . . . . . . . . . . . . . . . . . . . . . .205
**Appendix "A": It's Great to be a Buckeye** . . . . . . . . . . . 207
**Appendix "B": Have Tom Levenick Speak
    to your group** . . . . . . . . . . . . . . . . . . . . . . . . . . . . 213

# ABOUT THE AUTHOR

### BACKGROUND

- Tom Levenick graduated in Journalism from The Ohio State University in 1984. He is a former Ohio State football player, having played for Woody Hayes and Earle Bruce and on three bowl teams – The 1978 Gator Bowl, 1980 Rose Bowl, and 1981 Fiesta Bowl. He also was a finisher in the 1989 Hawaiian Ironman Triathlon World Championship. Levenick went on to assume many Vice President level leadership positions with companies such as The Winterbrook Beverage Group, Coors Brewing Company, Labatt USA and now, President of PowerPlay Strategies.

### PREVIOUS WRITING

- Tom has written for the Lantern, the Ohio State University Newspaper in 1983-84, The Ohio Business journal, and he has written columns for the Buckeyegrove.com website in 2013, 2014, & 2015.

# TOM LEVENICK

"Buckeyes for Life"

## Tom Levenick

- *Ohio State Football 1978 – 1982*
- *Ohio State Letter winner 1978, 1979*
- *Gator Bowl, Rose Bowl, Fiesta Bowl Team*
- *1989 Hawaiian Ironman Finisher*
- *Ohio State Varsity "O" Alumni Association Board of Directors – 2018-2020*

1979 Tackles and Tight Ends          Tom Levenick

# PRAISES FOR BUCKEYES FOR LIFE

*"Tom Levenick is a great writer and a great Buckeye. He continually "Pays Forward" for The Ohio State University and Buckeye Football. Buckeyes for Life is a great inspirational book that will be a treasure to Buckeye fans around the world."*

**Alan Brady**
*Ohio State Lacrosse 1972 – 1976*
*President Emeritus – The Varsity "O" Alumni Association*


*"Buckeyes for Life is a terrific compilation of behind the scenes stories about the things that make Ohio State football the most elite program in college football today. Tom has done a masterful job of unveiling the passion that exists within the "Buckeye Brotherhood" of former players. Buckeye Nation and college football fans in general will love this read.*

**Jim Lachey**
*Ohio State Football 1981 – 1984*
*First-team All-American 1984*

# TOM LEVENICK

*"Tom Levenick played for Woody Hayes and Earle Bruce and is himself a "Buckeye for Life." All Buckeye fans will love the inspirational "behind the scenes" stories that Tom shares. This is a terrific book."*

**Archie Griffin**

Ohio State Football 1972 – 1975
Two Time Heisman Trophy Winner
Two Time Big Ten Most Valuable Player
Former CEO of The Ohio State University Alumni Association


*"Buckeyes for Life is a wonderful look at college sports from the inside. Whether you are a Buckeye fan or college football fan, Tom Levenick does a wonderful job of ensuring this book is for everyone who enjoys college football. He is a master at story telling; you will laugh, smile, and may cry at times. Get ready to go the length of the football field in Buckeyes for Life and learn about what makes The Ohio State Buckeyes one of the top college football programs in the country."*

**Cardiff D. Hall**

Graduate of The Ohio State University – 1991
BSBA Major in Logistics and Marketing.
The Ohio State University Marching Band "I" Dotter 1990
Author of Tide Turners and President Inspiration Insight

# DEDICATION

Thanks to Dr. David Andrews, my Neurosurgeon at Thomas Jefferson University Hospital in Philadelphia. Dr. Andrews performed my brain surgery September of 2016 and without him, I may not have been able to write this book you are about to read. He has referred me to the Chief of Neurosurgery at the James Comprehensive Cancer Hospital at The Ohio State University, where I will continue to get terrific care. Hence a percentage of the proceeds from this book going to the Urban and Shelley Meyer Cancer Research Fund at the James.

To all of the former Ohio State Players of the "Buckeye Brotherhood:" Thanks for giving freely of your time and shedding tears of inspiration, joy and laughter with me, while we relived many stories of our past and present lives and how they were impacted by being a part of the incredible culture of the football program at The Ohio State University. *You are the best* and it is great that deep down in our hearts, we are all *"Buckeyes for Life."*

**Dr. David Andrews**
Director, Division of Neuro-oncologic Neurosurgery and Stereotactic Radiosurgery
Thomas Jefferson University Hospital

# ACKNOWLEDGEMENTS

I could not have written this book without the help of Alan Brady, Rick Smith, and Larry Romanoff, who all selflessly gave their time and effort to help me connect with some great Buckeyes with whom I had lost touch.
It is great to be reconnected as we are all
*"Buckeyes for Life!"*
Thank you also to Cardiff Hall, former member of "The Best Damn Band in the Land" and "I Dotter" of the Incomparable Script Ohio at the 1990 Michigan Game. Cardiff's motivation has been a great help as well as his introduction of me to Kary Oberbrunner at Author Academy Elite. I thank Kary and his team for their coaching and professionalism in helping me publish **"Buckeyes for Life."** I also thank Rob Cleveland from The Ohio State University Department of Trademarks and Licensing for his guidance regarding the likenesses in this book.
Writing this book has not just been a labor of love, it has been one of the greatest experiences of my life. While I have spoken to nearly 50 former Buckeye Athletes, Coaches, and band members, each discussion has been enlightening, inspirational, moving, and sometimes quite humorous. Each time I hung up the telephone, I had tears running down my cheeks, either from an inspirational story or from laughing until I cried. There are many stories that I have chosen not to publish as they are somewhat "off color" and after reading

them, some readers might team up to have me excommunicated from the "Buckeye Nation." However, there could be a second version that I publish, called "Buckeyes for Life Uncensored!"

I hope all the readers of ***"Buckeyes for Life"*** find this issue an enjoyable read, which gives them an inspirational and fun look behind the scenes of Ohio State Athletics. **It has been my honor to write it for you.**

# INTRODUCTION

*To the Best Damn Fans in the Land, this book is for you!*

***Buckeyes for Life*** is written in honor of the bond of former Ohio State football athletes that are extraordinary and have transcended the generations. It is amazing to witness this "Buckeye Brotherhood" in action, when you see teammates from every decade going back to the 1940s, staying in touch, connected tightly, often coming to the aid of a teammate in need or giving a "pat on the back" during a celebratory moment in their lives. I believe this environment was created from Woody Hayes' philosophies that "You Win with People" and you should always "Pay Forward." Despite numerous referrals by former players to stories and teachings by Woody Hayes, this is not intended to be a total "Woody book."

Additionally, while this is predominantly about Ohio State Football, there is a prevailing cascade of this culture throughout Ohio State athletics in general and I have relayed thoughts, stories, and experiences from letter winners in men's basketball, track and field, golf, women's basketball, women's swimming, and The Ohio State University Marching Band.

This culture has also begun to expand to the overall Ohio State University society. Simply go to the Ohio State University Alumni Association internet site and find the section under membership where you can "Pay Forward."

Let's face it. Life is a competition. You compete for positions and promotions at work. You compete for the best parking spot. You compete for the best spot in the checkout lane at the grocery store. You compete for the best table at a restaurant. You compete to have the best-looking lawn in your neighborhood. On and on and on! There are many social elements within this book that facilitate The Ohio State Buckeyes being the best competitors and winners possible. These elements and characteristics, when applied to everyday life, will foster success and wonderful life fulfillment.

I am so proud to be a graduate of The Ohio State University and I am even more gratified and fulfilled to be a member of the **"Buckeye Brotherhood"** and a **"Buckeye for Life."**

A recent experience with brain surgery and brain cancer, which I am still battling today, has precipitated this book. The outpouring of prayers, care, and concern from my "Buckeye Brothers" has been incredible and extremely gratifying.

My current experience with brain cancer also inspired me to donate a percentage of the proceeds from this book to the Urban and Shelley Meyer Cancer Research Fund at the James, Ohio State's Comprehensive Cancer Center.

While the "Buckeye Brotherhood," "Winning with People," and "Paying Forward" have transcended the generations at Ohio State and have been passed from Woody to Earle Bruce, John Cooper, Jim Tressel, and now Urban Meyer. Coach Meyer embodies those philosophies and has taken them to a new level.

# 1

## "YOU WIN WITH PEOPLE"

Woody Hayes wrote a book titled, "You Win with People," in 1973 and he sure did!

I had some very memorable experiences early on, from my "high school recruiting experience through my first three years at The Ohio State University, that molded my life forever.

While I was being recruited as a senior at Washington Community High School in Washington, Illinois (Population – 6,000) I was in the stage of recruiting where interested university head football coaches would make in home visits in order to sell the parents and family on their son attending their respective university as a destination for their son to earn his college degree *and* play football as a student athlete.

At that time, Dan Devine, head coach at Notre Dame; Bob Cummings of the University of Iowa; Bill Mallory of the University of Colorado; and Gary Moeller, head coach of the University of Illinois, had all been to the house.

Then, Dave Adolph, defensive coordinator at The Ohio State University and subsequently coach with the San Diego Chargers, Cleveland Browns, and Oakland Raiders called on a Monday and said he and Coach Woody Hayes would like to stop by the house Thursday to visit with my parents and me.

I asked my mother if that would be okay and she said, "Absolutely not!" She said, "I have seen him throwing sideline markers on the field and punching cameramen and I will not have that heathen in my home!"

I was devastated! I had always respected Ohio State and Woody Hayes was one of the greatest coaches ever! I corralled my dad in the den, away from my mom, and I begged him to lobby with my mom to allow Coach Adolph and Coach Hayes to come for a visit that upcoming Thursday. My dad prevailed and my mom then acquiesced and allowed coaches Adolph and Hayes to come for a visit that Thursday.

Then, the big snow of 1978 happened! I was worried that Adolph and Woody weren't going to be able to make it after all my consternation.

Two days later, it was the Thursday when Adolph and Woody were supposed to be making their visit. Dave Adolph called and said they were still coming and to expect them around 7 pm.

That Thursday evening I was nervous, peering out the windows, awaiting their arrival when I then saw them pull up in their car in front of the house.

We had a steep driveway to our home and when they got out of the car, Adolph grabbed Woody by the arm to help him up the steep driveway, given we had nearly two feet of snow. I prayed to God that Woody not fall and break a hip on our driveway, thus making national news.

They made it to the front door and we welcomed them into our home. We had a red ceramic tile foyer in our home with a turning staircase up to the second floor to the bedrooms. Woody sat down on the first three steps of that staircase and removed his large black rubber gollashes.

Woody and Adolph then came into the living room of our home, fireplace ablaze, and my mother served coffee and coffee cake. In attendance were Woody, Adolph, my mother and father, me and my brother John, who had recently graduated from the University of Minnesota, earning his Master's Degree in psychology.

When we sat down, Woody broke out a book by Robert G. Ingersoll, who he promptly told us was his most favorite orator and who also happened to have lived in Peoria, Illinois, just 12 miles from where we were sitting. He then asked if he could read his favorite Ingersoll passage, which was the eulogy to his brother's grave in 1876. Woody opened the book and began: "Like an armed warrior, like a plumed knight, James G. Blaine marched down the halls of the American Congress and threw his shining lances full and fair against the brazen foreheads of every defamer of his country and maligner of its honor." Then he closed the book and recited the rest of the passage from memory with eloquence and style. I saw the surprise in my parent's eyes as they looked at one another.

Woody then began to discuss metallurgical properties with my dad, who was a senior metallurgical engineer at the Caterpillar Tractor Company. He then moved to my brother, John, who had recently earned his Master's Degree in psychology at the University of Minnesota, and began discussing elements of psychology. They were both amazed at the breadth of knowledge of this "Neanderthal" football coach.

What they didn't know was that Woody's father was the high school principal and superintendent at Newcomerstown High School in Newcomerstown, Ohio and that Woody placed a huge value on education. Woody himself had earned his bachelor's degree in Physical Education, another bachelor's degree in English and a Master's Degree in World War II History.

Woody then turned his attention to my mother and asked her, "Mrs. Levenick, how do you raise such wonderful sons?"

My mom, with tears in her eyes, answered, "With a lot of love Coach, a lot of love."

Woody answered in a manner he used quite often, "mhhm, Mhhm, mhhm…..that's what I thought you'd say."

We all stood to say our goodbyes. Woody asked me what I thought the percentage was of my decision to accept a scholarship to The Ohio State University and I said, "Coach, I am 95% sure I will be coming to Ohio State." Woody said, "Do you think you could make that 98%?"

I said, "Sure coach, consider it 98%." He said, "I want you to shake my hand on that right now." I shook his hand and I still had one more paid recruiting visit to Notre Dame that weekend. As Woody and Dave Adolph walked out the door to leave, Woody yelled back, "Don't let them "Golden Dome" you at Notre Dame this week!" That weekend, I visited the University of Notre Dame, met Head Coach Dan Devine and his staff and toured the campus. While the Irish "wined and dined" me, I returned home to Washington, Illinois with The Ohio State University still at the top of my list. As soon as I walked in the door, the phone rang. It was Woody. "Well, are you at 100% now and coming to Ohio State?"

I told him that I hadn't spoken with my family yet and asked him if he could call back. Woody told me to go talk with my parents and that he would call me back. I went and sat down with my mom and dad and told them that I planned to accept a scholarship and attend The Ohio State University. Woody called back in five minutes and I told Coach Hayes the news and he was thrilled and said "Congratulations on becoming a BUCKEYE!" When I got off the phone my brother Stu congratulated me and said, "I'll root for you in every game you play but one, Ohio State versus Illinois."

Time went by and since my mom and dad had not been to Columbus, Ohio or The Ohio State University, we decided to go to the Ohio State Spring Football Game, which was in Mid-April, 1978. While watching the game, Assistant Athletics Director Larry Romanoff stopped by and let us know that after the game there would be a barbecue at the French Field House, honoring the 1968 National Championship Team on the tenth Anniversary of their championship.

When we entered the French Field House, I immediately caught sight of many Ohio State and NFL Greats from "The 68 Team," players such as Jack Tatum, Rex Kern, John Brockington, Jim Otis, Jan White, and Jim Stillwagon. I was star struck. Suddenly, Woody Hayes appeared and came right up to greet my parents and me. He told my parents that he understood they had never been to Ohio State before and offered to give them a personal tour of the campus.

"Oh no", my mother said. "We couldn't have you do that Coach Hayes. Especially with the Anniversary Celebration and all your former players here."

"I insist", Woody said.

The next thing you know, he's loading my mom and dad into the passenger side of his El Camino truck and off they go! I was left behind to hang out with the likes of Jack Tatum, Rex Kern, John Brockington, Jim Otis, Jan White, and Jim Stillwagon. It was an awesome afternoon for an 18-year-old kid.

As my career developed at Ohio State, I was on the "Scout Team" my freshman year, running opponents plays against the starters, which meant the only contribution I made to the team was the harder I practiced, the better the starters became. Woody was then fired after the "Gator Bowl Incident," where he punched a player on the Clemson University team, our Gator Bowl opponent.

Earle Bruce was then hired as the head coach and I played for him my sophomore year. I played left offensive tackle for the Buckeyes that year. I played in every game, we went 11-0 and went to the Rose Bowl.

My Junior year I played for the Ohio State Buckeyes and Earle Bruce and I earned the starting left tackle position. We were just beginning the season when I suffered a very serious knee injury. It was called an "Unholy Triad," which means that everything had been torn away, but the bone. Earle Bruce brought the entire offensive team to visit me in the hospital that night and they made a ceremonial presentation to me of the "Yellow Jersey," which is the jersey color you are required to wear at practice if you are injured. I was scheduled to have major knee surgery the next morning at 7 am.

Unbeknownst to me, my mother was flying to Columbus that evening so she could be with me in the hospital after my surgery. The next morning, I was taken down for surgery as scheduled at 7 am.

When I awoke from surgery, still groggy from anesthesia, I looked to the foot of my bed and there was my mother, standing with Woody Hayes, who had his arm around her.

I had been a "Peon" on the Scout Team for Woody and he hadn't been my coach for three years. Yet here he was at the foot of my bed, three years later, comforting my mother and me. I was in the hospital seven days. There was no arthroscopic surgery back then as I had a cast from my hip to my toe. Woody came to see me every day. He washed my back, he brought me assignments from my classes and when I could get up on crutches, he took me up to see terminal cancer patients in the cancer ward, hoping to raise their spirits. One of those people in the cancer ward was Ernie Godfrey, a former player at Ohio State in 1914 and Woody's kicking coach from 1958 to 1961. That is the essence of the culture of Ohio State Buckeye Football. **Buckeyes for life!**

Fast forward 27 years to 2004. My father had been diagnosed with terminal cancer and my two brothers and I were moving my mother and father into a smaller home that would be more manageable for them. We were loading a moving truck with furniture and appliances, when my father grabbed me by the shirt sleeve and said, "Come here Tom, I want to show you something". He led me through the kitchen, back to that red ceramic tile foyer. We walked to the front door and at the base of the steps that rose upstairs to the bedrooms, was a small oriental rug.

My father slid the oriental rug aside and underneath that rug were two white footprints. My father said, "You know Tom, 27 years ago, when Woody came to visit and removed his gollashes here, the saltwater from his gollashes left these two imprints in the wax on the floor. Your mother has never waxed this section of the foyer ever again!". **Buckeyes for Life!!!!!**

## Marty Bannister, former ESPN Broadcaster, has his own experiences "Winning with People:

"My son Corey is a wounded warrior, having been wounded in Iraq. He has been admitted to Walter Reed National Military Medical Center in Bethesda, MD. I am there visiting with him and comforting him, when during his third day of residence at the hospital, the phone on his night stand rings. Corey answers the phone and looks at me with eyes as big as silver dollars. I patiently wait for him to finish his conversation, when I look at my watch and realize that 45 minutes has passed. Corey finally finishes his conversation and hangs up the phone. When I asked him who had called, he responded, 'Jim Tressel.'

"Years later, I got Corey on the sideline for the Penn State football game in 2008. That was the year he was injured. After the game—that was the one they lost. Remember, Pryor fumbled late in the game, ...13 to 6 was the final score of that game. We're in the locker room. I'm gearing up to do all my post-game interviews for the radio network and all the players came in. Almost one by one, they stopped and shook Corey's hand and apologized that they weren't able to win the game for him.

"I'll tell you, Tom, I still get choked up talking about it. It was really something else. My eyes were softball sized. My son just looked at me. He didn't expect any of that. Then Coach Tressel came in and stopped and talked to him before he went in to talk to the team for his post-game speech.

Probably for a good 10-12 minutes, he just grabbed my son and talked to him.

"Again, years later, Tressel was being inducted into the Ohio State Athletics Hall of Fame. He came up to me. When I saw him prior to the game, I hadn't seen him since he'd been let go at Ohio State. The first thing he said to me was, 'Hey, how's Sargent Bannister? How's Corey? How's he doing?' He didn't skip a beat. He remembered his name, everything. 'How's he doing. How is he? Is he doing great? Tell him I said hello. Tell him we're thinking about him.' Just remarkable stuff. That is what being a Buckeye is all about."

# 2
# "RECRUITING THE BUCKEYE WAY"

Obviously, Wayne Woodrow "Woody" Hayes believed in people and "Winning with People." He went out of his way to make people feel appreciated, valued, and respected, which led to great confidence and success for the Ohio State football program.

Among all the elements of maintaining an elite college football program, none are more important than the people philosophy, especially as it applies to recruiting, which is the lifeblood of college football.

## CHARACTER

Woody always believed that the first element you looked for in a recruit or potential Buckeye was character and that certainly began with the player and his family. Woody would pay special attention to how the player interacted with family and would also inquire about the player's character and integrity with high school coaches, teachers, and superintendents. He believed that players with incredible athletic skills, who also possessed terrific character and integrity, always built championship teams. That belief and philosophy has cascaded through generations at Ohio State and was continued by head coaches Earle Bruce, Jim Tressel, and Urban Meyer today.

## Urban Meyer

- Ohio State Grad Assistant Coach – 1986, 1987
- Illinois State Outside Linebacker Coach – 1988
- Colorado State Wide Receiver Coach – 1990, 1995
- Notre Dame Wide Receiver Coach – 1996 - 2000
- Bowling Green Head Football Coach – 2001, 2002
- Utah Head Football Coach – 2003, 2004
- Florida Head Football Coach – 2005, 2010
- Ohio State Head Football Coach – 2012-Present

- **CHAMPIONSHIPS**

    o 3 National – 2006, 2008, 2014
    o 2 MWC – 2003, 2004
    o 2 SEC – 2006, 2008
    o 1 Big Ten – 2014
    o 2 Big Ten Leaders – 2012, 2013
    o 1 Big Ten East Division – 2014

## Doug Plank gives his opinions on recruiting at Ohio State

"Here is what I think. Number one, I think if there is a tremendous amount, if you just level the playing field right now, would it take time for Ohio State to establish itself? Yes, it would. But it's the people that have been there before, I don't even know how to explain it. It's like you're recruiting athletes and trying to get out there and do the job. But somewhere, somehow, down there below the surface, this university, this coaching staff across a lot of different sports have done an incredible job of finding those people that life matters to them. They are not just people who are trying to go out there and try to get a scholarship, go play somewhere, go try to move on to the next level and make money, whatever. There is something about the quality of the athletes they have been able to recruit and have within their organization that makes them what they are. I didn't make Ohio State, I didn't even add one little teeny little smidgen to it, it was already there when I got there. I never ever thought about Ohio State even being an option for me at high school because it was up the stratosphere. They had just won a national championship a couple of years earlier, that was the closest thing you could get to the ability of the pros. Their programs spoke for itself, and that's why when the opportunity came—everything in life you can say, "You have got to take advantage of all your opportunities.

"You know what though? Those certain opportunities come within a very small window and if you don't take it at that time, it's gone. It's like you're going to the shopping market, you are going to the grocery, and they keep changing their stock all the time, they don't have the same bananas or fruits or choices that they have every week, it's almost like Costco or something. You go there, if you don't take advantage of this at this time, it's going to be gone for the rest of your life, and it's flashing right in front of you. That's the same as with

Ohio State, when we hear you say—you're going to get that champion to come to Ohio State by offering a scholarship, that was it.

"It wasn't any more difficult than that. I know there were some stories out there, that I had been sending letters to Joe Paterno and all that sort of thing. Joe Paterno, they had a good program at Penn State, they were winning a lot of games. But it wasn't like Ohio State, and sometimes when you grow up and you're a young kid, you're scared of going any place. I've only been outside the state of Pennsylvania twice in my whole life as a senior in high school. So, the safe choice was to go to Penn State. That was where everybody else went that lived in the area.

"But I think it's a job that Ohio State can do in terms of attracting, not only kids that are talented, but the right kids, and the tradition.

"There was an event out here in Arizona where I was at one of the games down here and Ohio State was playing in it. I had a chance to meet some of the other athletes who had played in different sports for Ohio State over the years.

"I was just talking to them. One girl in particular was on the female swim team from the state of Illinois. I asked her, I said, 'What in the world made you choose Ohio State over another school?' I said, 'What was it?' She said, 'I came to a football game.' She said, 'I've never seen anything like that in my life.' She said, 'That made my decision.' I said, 'So you came to a football game to make a decision, you then go to Ohio State to swim?' She goes, 'Yes. I can't explain it. I couldn't explain it to my parents. Way back in the day, I'm just telling you, Doug, today, here, right now. That's what it was. That's what made the difference.'

"I've never ever heard anybody ever say anything like that from a cross sports standpoint, 'Yes, I went to play football there because they had a great baseball team or a great basketball team,' and she said, 'That was just the people that were there. The support, I've never seen anything like it.' I try to explain sometimes when I go to other schools and other places. You always want to be respectful of all schools, their alumni, and all that sort of thing. I just say, 'You don't have to say anything about the event. It speaks for itself.'

"The first game," Doug said, "we grew up in Pennsylvania; Western Pennsylvania, just outside of Pittsburgh we're huge Pitt fans, Steeler fans, Penn State fans. My mother comes in the first game and just sits in the stands. Afterwards, she still had tears in her eyes.

"We won the game. It was not anything, we were not expected to win. We did win 56 – 0 or something. She goes, 'Doug, I'm just still trying to get a hold of myself,' and I said, 'Why?' She goes, 'I have never seen anything like the band coming out on the field like that.' And she said, 'I just started crying uncontrollably.'

"I went, 'What?' She was, 'Yes, I just couldn't control myself, I don't know what it was.'

"But I think you add up all those things and on top of it, it's great tradition of the school and all of the other factors. I just think it's not a normal course of what you would expect out of life and we maybe have become too accustomed to going other places where they have good teams and great things happen and all that sort of thing. But, I don't know, there's just something about Ohio State, the tradition, the players. To me—I don't know, when I came in they didn't have the greatest facilities at that time. Obviously, The Woody Hayes Center wasn't built. It was still the Ernie Biggs North Athletic facility when I was there. Better than most schools, but not like today.

"It was like, 'This looks okay, but it's not like a palace.' However, this place is special and the people that are there are very special and it's not about you, it's about this place and you will be spending four years of your life coming through those doors—hopefully, all you can do is add to it in some small part, some small way that maybe you left a little footprint there and say, 'This had a huge impact on my life, it really did, it gave me direction and the guys that had come out of there were so successful.'

"The other thing that just blew me away too was even like I remember while at practices, players that had been there within the last 10 years would show up at different times, pre-game, practice, all that. And just give a talk to the players, that got me motivated. They would take us back and say, "I remember when I was here practicing on Tuesdays, Wednesdays and Thursdays, getting ready for games." Wow, it's like these guys that you see on television, now they are right in front of you telling their story. It's like, that's powerful. And it's just how humble they were to have played at Ohio State and been part of it." ***Buckeyes for Life!***

## Doug Plank

- Ohio State Football 1971 – 1974
- Backup Strong Safety 1972 – 1974
- Chicago Bears 1975 – 1984
- Chicago Bears Starting Strong Safety 1975 – 1984
- Led Bears in tackles 1975

**Harold Brown was part of my recruiting class, the freshman class of 1978 at Ohio State, but Harold's recruitment and subsequent college career were unusual, to say the least.**

Harold was a gifted athlete and a phenomenal football player. As a halfback at Kent Roosevelt High School, Harold was a member of the Parade All American team. This was before the days of four-star and five-star recruits and the Parade All-American Team was the highest honor a high school player could receive. As a classic example of the level of that honor, the other running back on the 1977 Parade All American team was none other than Oakland Raider Star and future NFL Hall of Famer, Marcus Allen. His coach at Roosevelt, John Nemec, who developed over 30 Division 1 college players, said Brown was head and shoulders above them all. "Think of a bigger O.J. Simpson, that's how Harold ran."

Harold was being recruited by all the college football powers like Ohio State, Michigan, USC, UCLA, Penn State and Notre Dame. All the coaches were gracing the Halls at Kent Roosevelt and attending Harold's games, until the sixth game of Brown's senior season, when Harold broke his neck. Coach Nemec saw the X-rays the night of the injury and said he almost fell over when he saw how the broken bone had turned sideways in Harold's neck. He had no idea how bad Harold was hurt. No one did then.

Then, all of those coaches disappeared and stopped visiting Kent Roosevelt to see Harold, except one, Ohio State Head Football Coach Woody Hayes. None of those other schools bothered to pick up a phone. Woody even visited Harold in the hospital, where he told Harold, "I was recruiting you before you were injured and I am recruiting you after you've been injured. You have a full four-year scholarship to The Ohio State University.

Harold attended Ohio State as a member of our class, but could never practice in full pads. He came to practice every day in sweats and ran sprints and some agility drills, but that was all he was allowed. Brown redshirted one year at Ohio State, where he also placed fifth in the long jump at the Big 10 indoor track meet. We used to have "pickup" basketball games in St. John Arena during the off season, with some current players against some of the past players like Brian Baschnagel, Fred Pagac, Craig Cassady, Art Schlichter, Doug Donley, and others.

I will never forget Harold bringing the ball down the court on a fast break and "slam dunking" the ball and slapping both hands on the backboard as he came down.

Earle Bruce was the Head Coach for our sophomore year, but had to let Harold go at the direction of team doctors once he saw his medical records (Harold had 3 vertebrae fused).

Brown spent time away and then went to junior college at Joliet in Illinois where he set a new NJCAA rushing record in 1981 with 2274 yards on 298 carries.

Earle Bruce made arrangements for him to play a year at Iowa State, where Earle was the head coach prior to Ohio State. Harold shared the running back position with another guy, but he did win Big 8 Player of the Week once for a game against Kent State, where he rushed for nearly 250 yards.

The Washington Redskins drafted him—this coming off their Super Bowl win with John Riggins—but cut him after two preseason games. The reason was the liability and risk of further serious injury.

Harold is currently teaching History at Wassan High School in Colorado Springs, Colorado.

I spoke to Harold recently and he had said he wouldn't change a thing. **"Buckeyes for Life".**

Harold Brown

**Eric Kumerow shares some recruiting thoughts:**

I am a Buckeye for life and I bleed Scarlet and Gray, I watch every game. I'm sure you're aware, that the Bosa Boys are my nephews. When they were recruiting Joey, I was getting calls from Coach Meyer and I was willing to do anything and everything I could to try and help them land those kids. But it really didn't take much more than my sister being an alumni, you know what I mean? So, I don't think it's really anything that I said or did to get them there. But boy, it looks like Nicky is going to have to have a similar career as Joey. There's a certain brotherhood that forms when you're making a commitment to play a game like college football, especially at Ohio State. The big games, the tough losses, the big wins. I mean, it's just a part of your life that should never be replaced no matter what you go on and do. You can't replace that. **"Buckeyes for Life"**

 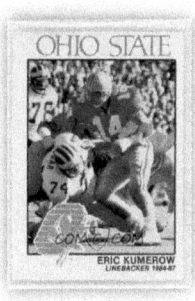 

# ERIC KUMEROW

- Ohio State Football 1984 – 1987
- Ohio State Starting Defensive End – 1986, 1987
- Miami Dolphins – 1988-1990
- Chicago Bears – 1991

**Kirk Herbstreit shares his recruiting story:**

I wanted to go to Ohio State my whole life. My high school senior year was 1987, the fall of '87, and Earl got fired that year right in the middle of me being recruited. John Cooper was announced head coach, I think December 31st of '87. I committed to him. I was so tired of lying to Penn State in Michigan and USC and all these other schools. I was ready to commit to Ohio State and as soon as they announced John Cooper, I told them, "I'm coming."

## KIRK HERBSTREIT

- Ohio State Football 1988 – 1992
- Ohio State – Four-year letter winner at quarterback
- Ohio State starting Quarterback – 1992
- Ohio State Team Captain – 1992
- ESPN College Gameday Analyst – 1994-Present

**Tim Burke shares a great recruiting experience as a future Buckeye:**

My senior year at Wapakoneta High School in Wapakoneta, Ohio, I am being recruited by Miami of Ohio, Michigan State, Notre Dame, Penn State, and some other schools. I don't know why, but it seemed like all the college coaches would come to see me right after lunch at my school. I had geometry class right after lunch and my teacher was Mrs. Ford. I needed this class for college credit. We had an intercom system or speaker system that went through the entire school and when a college coach came to visit me, our principal, we called him Bud, but Mr. Marshall, would get on the mic and say: "Tim Burke please report to the office". I was always in Mrs. Ford's room and I was getting called out like every day, every other day.

She calls me inside and tells me, "If you miss one more math class because all of these football recruiters think you're going to play football—you won't be playing football because I'll fail you. One more class, I'm failing you."

So, I go to my head football coach John Nemick. I said, "Nemo, Ms. Ford says if I miss one more class she'll fail me." He went and talked to her. She's like, no, because she was not afraid of him. She said, "He's not going to miss another class or I'm going to fail him". Okay. So in the end it went out that any coaches that to see me had to wait until Mrs. Ford's class was over and then they could call me to the office. Okay, no problem.

So, one day a couple weeks later, Bud Marshall gets on the PA and says, "Tim Burke, please report to the office". Ms. Ford's up at the board writing. She stops writing, turns and glances over her shoulder. I'm shaking my head sideways like, "Nope. No way. Don't worry about it I ain't going nowhere." Two minutes later, "Tim Burke, please report to the office." Now she's frustrated and I'm shaking my head, no.

Two minutes later, outside the door, and there's a little glass window. Like three feet tall by one foot wide. It's kind of a weird door. I see Bud Marshall walk up, he's knocking on the door while she's at the board writing. She lays the chalk down, she goes to open the door. She opens it and he goes, "Step out here, I need to talk to you." I'm like, "What the hell is going on?" She steps out, I'm looking through the window, Bud's talking, and she's shaking her head, no, and moving her arms and he keeps being really dramatic. He wasn't that way. Talking the same things that, finally she drops her head. She turns around, she opens the door, she said, "Go on." I said, "You told me that if I left one class, for whatever reasons, if I left the class, you're going to fail me."

She said, "Woody Hayes is downstairs and he wants to see you right now." I had been getting recruited by Kentucky, Indiana, Penn State, Notre Dame, but of course, many of the boys immediately recognized that it was Woody Hayes and it spread like wildfire. Half of them jumped up and ran to the office. There's mayhem going on. That's how Bud Marshall found out Woody Hayes was in the building because he came in through the cafeteria. The whole school is in an uproar. I'm thinking, mistake, not a mistake? Woody knows I'm from a small town lower white redneck middle class family. Dad's an electrician, mom stays at home, baking bread with children. There were no high school diplomas for either one of them. A few hours later, I'm walking down the hall and I look into an office and there is Mrs. Long sitting down, talking with Woody Hayes.

I'm not Tom Cousineau, I'm not Rod Gerald, I'm not Jimmy Moore, I'm not getting recruited *by every* school in the country. The only other visit Woody Hayes made to Wapakoneta—I don't know how much later it was than this, came one day, when I got home from school and I walk in the house, mom has made some bacon bread and she's got some brownies that she made there and she goes, "Guess who was here today?" I'm looking around and I ask if it was my aunts and I said, "You've been baking bread, I thought maybe they'd come over and help you." She said, "No, it's somebody that was really important." I'm like, "Okay, I don't know." She said, "Coach Woody Hayes was here and he told me that those brownies he ate were the best brownies he had ever eaten in his life." She says, "I'm going to tell you something, I can sit down right there. That man, he's going to take care of you and he's going to watch out for you.

"I don't have to worry about you because you get in trouble. You're going to have to answer to him, just like your dad. You're going to go to Ohio State."

How anybody knew Coach Hayes came to the Western Buckeye League to see Tim Burke, I'm now getting letters from Bear Bryant, and from Joe Paterno, that I've never gotten, they didn't even know I was alive. Woody Hayes comes and within a month, I'm now getting the introductory letters and being asked to come and make a visit at a handful of a bigger universities. I'm now hearing from all of the other Big Ten schools immediately.

I look back and laugh. He came to realize real quickly, especially once you met my mom, that she ran the household. He knew my background. He knew the environment I grew up in and that a handshake meant everything. He locked me up and the entire community. My mom's like, "You're going to Ohio State."

So, my dad and I go down to Columbus to visit and Woody sets me down. He's talking to me and my Dad and he says, "Now we got great talent here, you're going to be part of that if you come here." He said, "You're not going to start your freshman year, you probably won't start your sophomore year, but if you work hard and you continue to improve and get stronger, which you will if you come here, you will, you could start your junior and senior year."

You'll be part of a great program. Then he said, "I want to offer you a full scholarship to The Ohio State University." He stuck his hand out and my dad's sitting right beside me in the chair and the reason he did that, was because he knew the way I was raised and that if I stand up and I shake that man's hand, this is done.

I'm thinking, oh my God, I'm going to go to Miami University and Michigan State was recruiting me and I was planning to take a visit there and if I shake his hand, I know my dad will tell me. I ain't going anywhere, I'm making no visits because this is done. About this amount of time, which was 30 seconds, my dad looked at me and said, "Boy, what are you going to do?" I stood up and I shook Coach Hayes hand.

On the way to home dad said, "Those coaches they are good guys. I'm sure there's good schools but you're going to call them all to thank them and tell them that they don't need to waste their time because you're a Buckeye. You're going Ohio State."

I had to call every one of the coaches from other schools that had reached out to me because some of them now are talking to me and tell them I'm going to Ohio State. It was the best decision I ever made!!!

## TIM BURKE

- Ohio State Football 1975 – 1979
- Left Offensive Tackle 1975, 76, 77, 78 & 79
- Starting Left Offensive Tackle 1979
- 1979 Rose Bowl Champion

While I (Tom Levenick) was being recruited in 1977 to attend The Ohio State University in 1978, Alex Gibbs, then the guard and center coach at Ohio State relayed a recruiting story to me about wide receiver, Doug Donley. Gibbs was the assistant coach recruiting Donley and he told me that he was taking Woody Hayes to Cambridge High School and Cambridge, Ohio to watch wide receiver recruit, Doug Donley, play a varsity basketball game for the Cambridge Bears. Woody loved watching recruits participate in other sports to observe their athleticism. This particular evening, Gibbs told Woody, "When you see Doug on the court, you may think he's too small to play at Ohio State, but he is a terrific athlete, with great character and a great family and a player we should have on our team. Doug at the time weighed 155 pounds. What they didn't know was that Doug had recently had surgery on his right shoulder. Doug was right handed, yet they taped and wrapped his right arm to his torso. He played the game as the starting point guard for the Bears, playing left handed and one handed and led the Bears to victory scoring 23 points." Woody was sold!

Then the time came for Woody's personal visit to the Donley home. "Woody came over to our house for dinner and I was pretty nervous," Donley said. "My recruiting choices were down to Notre Dame, Ohio State, and Michigan, and I didn't want things to go poorly. During dinner, the phone rang and my mom answered the phone and then came back to the table and said, 'Doug, the call is for you, but you should probably take this one in the back bedroom.' I left the table and went to take the call. The caller was none other than Bo Schembechler. I was polite, but understandably short with Coach Schembechler. I then went back to the dinner table, very nervous about Bo calling, hoping it would not come up during the conversation with Coach Hayes. No sooner had I sat down, when Woody asked, 'Who was that on the phone young man?' I stammered, 'Well Coach that was Bo Schembechler who called.' Woody stood up, walked to the head of the table and thrust his hand out to me and said, 'Young man, I want your commitment and handshake, here and now, that you will accept a full scholarship to play football and attend The Ohio State University.' I shook Woody's hand and the rest is history. I had a great career at Ohio State and then went on to some good years with the Dallas Cowboys and Chicago Bears."

## Doug Donley

- *Ohio State Wide Receiver 1977-1980*
- *Honorable Mention All American Wide Receiver 1980*
- *All Big Ten Wide Receiver 1979 & 1980*
- *Dallas Cowboys Wide Receiver 1981-1984*
- *Chicago Bears Wide Receiver 1986*

**Bill Lukens shares a unique recruiting story:**

"This story kind of shows what happened when you pushed Woody's buttons. When I was a senior at Ohio State, we were recruiting a big tight end from Cincinnati, named Mark Schmerge. He was a big dude and everybody was recruiting him. Since I was from Cincinnati, and Mark and I went to the same high school, I was the person that was assigned to be his player host and to help recruit him. Mark ended up going to Michigan, which was decided the night we went out to dinner with Woody for sure. So, we go out to dinner with Woody and Mark's dad, who was an orthopedic surgeon. Dr. Schmerge, for some reason, he hated Woody's guts. I'm not sure why that was. So, we are sitting down to dinner and Dr.

Schmerge started getting on Woody's case. He says, 'You know Woody, I don't like the way that you run your offense. I don't like the way you treat the press and I saw when you tore up those sideline markers, and I think your actions are disgusting.' All of a sudden, Woody stands up and says, 'You know, I don't care if you're a doctor and I don't care who your son is, because I don't like you either you son of a bitch!' I thought, well, I guess Mark isn't coming to Ohio State!"

## BILL LUKENS

- *Ohio State Offensive Guard 1973-1976*
- *Team Captain 1976*

# 3

## "PAYING FORWARD"

### (Ralph Waldo Emerson and Woody Hayes)

Woody Hayes used to teach us that "You can never pay back, you can only Pay Forward." He taught us that to mold our behavior in the community, philanthropically, and with friends and family. Quite often, when speaking to the TEAM about "Paying Forward," he would recite the following quote from Ralph Waldo Emerson and his Theory on Compensation: *"You can pay back only seldom. You can always pay forward, and you must pay line for line, deed for deed, and cent for cent." "You can never pay back; but you can always pay forward."*

Woody didn't just preach about Paying Forward. He exemplified it and demonstrated it most days of his life.

George Hill was the Defensive Coordinator for the Ohio State Buckeyes and Woody Hayes for eight years, 1970-1978. George related a story from his days as defensive coordinator for the Buckeyes, when his office was located next door to Woody's in St. John arena. "This would have been 1977," Hill said. "Woody knocked on my door and asked that I join him for lunch at the Faculty Club across campus. We walked across the oval and were seated at the same table Woody always occupied and we were served by a young college junior, who served Woody every time he had lunch at the Faculty Club. We had a great lunch, talking about our defense for the upcoming 1977 season, when our waitress brought the bill and told Coach Hayes that unfortunately she would not be able to wait on him anymore, because she was dropping out of school due to lack of finances. Woody asked her how many quarters she had left to complete her degree, to which she replied, three. Woody then said, 'You're not going to drop out of school. You come see me at St. John Arena tomorrow at 9:00 and we'll see what we can do about you finishing your education.'

"The young girl arrived at about 10 minutes before nine o'clock the next morning and I could see her pacing nervously outside Woody's office. Woody invited her in and closed the door. Thirty minutes passed by, then 45 and it was going on one hour, when the door opened and the young girl exited Woody's office with a handkerchief and had tears streaming down her face.

"I was a little worried," said Hill, "and I went in and asked Woody, 'Is everything alright Coach?' And Woody said, 'Yes, George everything is fine.' Then he said, 'You know George, back when we won the National Championship in 1957, the OSU Alumni Association gave me a Cadillac. I didn't need a goddamn Cadillac! I refused to accept it, but they said coach, it is already bought and paid for. I said, I don't care, let's do something different. So, they decided to sell it and give me the money. I told them that I would put that money in an account at the bank and that not one member of the Hayes family would ever see a nickel of that money.' Then, Hayes said, 'And you know what George, we win the National Championship again in 1961 and those dumb sons of bitches buy me another Cadillac! We went through the same exercise and sold the Cadillac and put those funds in the bank as well. Do you know George,' Woody said with that sly smile on his face. "We have now used that fund to help 73 different students complete their degrees at our wonderful Ohio State University.'

"That was in 1977, and Woody lived until 1987. No one will ever know how many people Woody helped from that one fund. "In addition to the countless other people we know he "Paid Forward" and supported throughout his life. It is incredible what a level of humanitarianism Wayne Woodrow 'Woody' Hayes maintained throughout his life and how many countless examples we uncover yet today." **Buckeyes for Life!!!!!**

## George Hill

- Ohio State Defensive Coordinator – 1971-1978
- Indianapolis Colts Defensive Coordinator – 1985-1988
- Miami Dolphins Linebacker Coach – 1989-1995
- Miami Dolphins Defensive Coordinator – 1996-1999

**"I firmly believe Pam Geist was one of the many recipients from 'Woody's Fund'," said Bill Jaco. Bill Jaco, a former Buckeye Teammate (Tight End & Tackle 1976-79) relayed the following "Paying Forward" story:**

"Jake" as we call him was being recruited by Woody after his senior season at Toledo St. Francis High School, where he played football, basketball and baseball for the Knights.

Pam Norman was the Valedictorian of the St. Francis senior class and later went on to be the roommate of Joan Jaco, Bill's wife of now 35 years.

The story evolved as Pam was being honored at a Lions Club function in Toledo that featured Woody Hayes as a keynote speaker. Geist had the opportunity and fortune to meet up with Coach Hayes that evening and Woody was enamored by Pam's intelligence, academic performance, and certainly with the fact that she planned to attend The Ohio State University. She was excited to be embarking on her academic career at Ohio State, but shared a concern with Woody, that her family was not financially stable and she worried about her ability to complete her education. Coach Hayes, in his ever-omnipresent manner, told Pam that if she ever needed any help, what so ever, to call him in his office at St. John Arena. He gave her his card and wrote his direct line phone number on the back.

Three years had gone by and despite part time work and college aid, Pam was at the end of her rope and was not going to be able to afford to complete her degree. She remembered that conversation with Coach Hayes and then asked Bill Jaco if he thought she should call Woody. Jake said "Absolutely, give him a call and I'm sure he will do whatever he can to help you." Pam called Coach Hayes and he instructed her to come visit him the next morning on campus. It was then that Woody confirmed to Pam that he would support her completion of her degree and provided her with a check to cover the last year of her college education. To this day, Bill Jaco believes that Coach Hayes provided one of the unused football athletic scholarships to fund her education. This was in the day when there were 120 scholarships allocated by NCAA rules versus the 85 scholarships which are allowed today.

Pam Norman went on to receive her bachelor's degree in Mathematics from The Ohio State University in 1979 and then went on to receive her master's degree in Mathematics

Education. After graduating and beginning to advance in life, Pam returned to visit Coach Hayes. She had written a check for the funds that Woody had advanced her and wanted to repay him for the wonderful deeds that he showered upon her. Woody would have no part of it. He told Pam to go out and "Pay Forward" to another student or individual who needed the same help that she did. Pam was amazed. "He was the most amazing man I ever met," Pam said. "He was incredibly educated, compassionate, and dedicated to helping other people. It changed my life forever." I firmly believe that Pam Geist was one of the many recipients from "Woody's Cadillac Fund". **Buckeyes for Life!**

## BILL JACO

- *Ohio State Football 1976-1979*
- *Tight End 1976 & 77*
- *Starting Tight End 1977*
- *Offensive Tackle and Tight End 1978 & 79*

**Randy Gradishar,** shared his thoughts on Paying Forward at Ohio State as well.

Gradishar was consensus All-American in 1972 and a unanimous All American in 1973, while also finishing sixth in the voting for the Heisman Trophy. He was also an Academic

All American and Woody Hayes called Gradishar "the greatest linebacker I ever coached." He is a member of the Ohio State Varsity "O" Hall of Fame and a member of the Ohio State All-Century Team.

"I had great experiences at Ohio State," Randy said. "Like beating Michigan in the greatest rivalry in all of sport. However, the greatest experience was the opportunity to play for Woody Hayes and learning to "Pay Forward." He taught me so much about character, integrity, discipline, accountability, respect, and fair play," Gradishar said. We would always visit children's hospitals and senior citizen's centers, showing care, learning to help, "Paying Forward," but not necessarily paying back," Gradishar has obviously learned well from his days with Woody and The Ohio State University. After all those college and NFL successes, Randy still resides in Colorado after his Bronco days. He has made trips to visit and support our troops in Iraq and Afghanistan; he was President of the Denver Broncos Youth Foundation, worked with Denver Promise Keepers and is the Honorary Chair for the Susan G. Kolmen Cure for Breast Cancer Foundation. **Buckeyes for Life!**

## RANDY GRADISHAR

- *Ohio State Football 1970-1973*
- *Ohio State Starting Linebacker 1971-1973*
- *Ohio State Varsity Hall of Fame*

- *Ohio State Football All-Century Team*
- *Denver Broncos 1973-1983*
- *7× Pro Bowl 1975, 1977-1979, 1981-1983*
- *2× First-team All-Pro 1977, 1978*
- *4× Second-team All-Pro 1973, 1981-1983*
- *7× All-AFC selection 1976-1979, 1981-1983*
- *NFL Defensive Player of the Year 1978*
- *2× All-American 1972, 1973*
- *Denver Broncos Ring of Fame*

**Cornelius Green is a firm believer in Paying forward and its contribution to the "Buckeye Brotherhood:"**

One reason why I feel that they have their players have such a bond is because of what I think Woody started back when he was coaching, making freshmen get in the van and going over to pay it forward, going over to hospitals visiting kids, sick kids. I can remember, I can recall vividly Archie and I became sick kids' favorite players and we went over, knowing that a kid might have had a week or two to live and we were their favorite player and we went over to meet that kid and became a good friend of that kid until his last days.

I think when you share bonds like that and pay the highest respect of life and then giving up your time and not being in that third person, so to speak, when you're speaking to third person and knowing who you really are as a man and a teammate. I think that's what means the world to be an Ohio State Player when you pay forward and for me particularly, in my life now, I'm in my last stages of my life and I'm paying forward by coaching here at St. Albert School football, basketball, and baseball head coach for the boarding school here paying forward.

BUCKEYES FOR LIFE

## A Facebook post by Cornelius Green – June 27, 2017

### Cornelius Green

I HAD A GREAT TIME IN GRAND RAPIDS. WE RAISE 5 GRAND FOR SCHOLARSHIPS FOR KIDS TO ATTEND THE OHIO STATE UNIVERSITY. GREAT JOB Donna Waters AND BARRY WATERS, Sonny Gordon GO, AND DAN LAVILLE. PAYING FORWARD IS SO REWARDING. I'M HEADING BACK HOME TO DC THIS MORNING. TRAVEL MERCIES PRAYERS PLEASE IN ADVANCE. GO BUCKS!!

### Cornelius Green

- Ohio State Football 1972-1975
- Big Ten Most Valuable Player (1975)
- 2× First-team All-Big Ten (1974-1975)

As you can see, the concept of Paying Forward, while it was embedded in the Ohio State Football program during the 1950s, 60s, and 70s, still resonates within the program, maybe at an even higher level today. Today, it actually resonates throughout the entire Ohio State University community and culture and has even expanded throughout much of the University.

**Archie Griffin, former Ohio State Great and two-time Heisman Trophy winner certainly believes in Paying Forward.**

After his playing days were over, Archie created the Archie Griffin Scholarship fund, which provides athletic scholarships to deserving, yet underprivileged student athletes from Ohio to The Ohio State University. The following is Archie's mission statement for the Archie Griffin Scholarship Fund: **People say good things come in threes. That may be. But for me, good things come in twos: two Heismans, two Diplomas.**

That's right. Earning an education ranks right up there with some of life's best rewards. My athletic ability afforded me a scholarship to get an education. I took advantage of that opportunity. My football playing days are over, but I use my education every day. Now with the support of several Columbus area corporations, I have an opportunity to offer others what I once received: an athletic scholarship. The Archie Griffin Scholarship Fund creates scholarship opportunities for high school scholar-athletes to attend The Ohio State University. We have 26 athletes right now on scholarship at Ohio State. I know that we've raised about a million and a half dollars or somewhere close to a million and a half dollars for the athletes today. The interest on that fund means I have provided for, that would be probably the number over the years without penance for life for over 20 years. It's been one of those labors of love more than anything.

## ARCHIE GRIFFIN

**Archie Griffin Scholarship Fund**

- Ohio State Football 1972 – 1975
- Maxwell Award (1975)
- 2× Heisman Trophy (1974, 1975)
- 2× Walter Camp Award (1974, 1975)
- 2× *Sporting News* Player of the Year (1974, 1975)
- 2× UPI Player of the Year (1974, 1975)
- 2× Big Ten Most Valuable Player (1973, 1974)
- 3× First-team All-American (1973–1975)
- 3× First-team All-Big Ten (1973–1975)
- Ohio State Buckeyes No. 45 retired

**Roy Hall, former Buckeye and Indianapolis Colt Receiver, has a terrific philosophy on "Paying Forward:"**

At the end of the day or the beginning of any type of purposeful walk, you have to start with where you come from. My mom did a great job of raising me pretty much by herself in a single parent household. Dad had some challenges with some drugs and some drug abuse issues. Him and my mom got divorced early and so his heroin addiction dictated a lot of what my mom was able to do with her kids, but my sister and I, just growing up, living check to check, not really having the finer things in life, so to speak, in the refrigerator, living check to check, like I said. Just being in the situation where my mom tried her best to do everything she could for my sister and I and watching my mom go through physical and emotional abuse, those were the things that made growing up very challenging. Not having your father in your household to teach you things that men are supposed to teach you.

I started playing organized football since the seventh grade because we couldn't really afford to do any type of camps or travel teams or anything like that. You kind of just learn to be athletic just by being in the streets with your friends. Your friends become your family, but you understood at an early age that life is not supposed to be like that. If you want to be great, you will have to sacrifice and just watching my mom's sacrifice year after year, day after day, to make sure that I had what I needed especially when I got to high school to be successful was awesome. Once I got in a position of influence at Ohio State learning that we're here for a greater purpose than just entertainment. We are playing ball, that and God has really blessed us with a platform to be used for a purpose to help build his kingdom through service.

Once I kind of got those values instilled in me at Ohio State I knew that I could make a difference long term and so when I got to the NFL, obviously, that really rearranged how I wanted to do things.

Because I knew I had a national platform. I had that NFL shield behind me and I could, outside of the state of Ohio, really make a difference and make an impact with the great sport of football. And being around Tony Dungy and Peyton Manning and Marvin Harris and Reggie Wayne and Dallas Clark and Jerry Bracket and all these great people that I played with in Indianapolis. I really saw how you can leverage people's affinity and love for football and use it to your advantage to help them and position them. Help the people in need that don't have that platform that you have.

In 2008, I started the Driven Foundation. I was rookie in the NFL, started off with just a football camp but five years ago when I got done playing ball, I really made it a priority and that's what I was called to do with my life. So now running the organization here in central Ohio we've been able to distribute over 650,000 pounds of free food to over 5,400 central Ohio families, have about six or seven mentorship programs running around the 270 Outerbelt. We do a lot of cool projects working on inner city families and even suburban families, different issues across the board. Speaking engagements and motivational inspirational speaking around the country. I actually just got back from Las Vegas doing a weekend KENO out there in the National Conference. So, me and my partner Antonio Smith who is also a former Buckeye, have been doing a great job with the organization and that's kind of how we got started and that's why we do what we do.

I'm really here to serve, nothing more, nothing less. We have a great partnership with the Ohio State football team currently and Coach Meyer, just a lot of service projects that we got coming up in the fall. And really that's what life is about.

I get tired of people talking about their ambitions and their goals and what they want to do with their life and what they want to accomplish and how much they want to have saved and how they want to leave a legacy for their family. That's cool and that's great but at the end of the day how are you positioning yourself to help people that don't have those opportunities to build a legacy, they can't build their own life, let alone build a legacy. So, these people that have multi-million dollars in the bank account that can go to these fancy country clubs and have these great conversations at their golf outings and in their business meeting and their CEO this and CEO that. But how are we really serving on a day-to-day basis is what I'm about. I'm not about the one time, I'll give something back on Thanksgiving or give something away on Christmas. Or I go to the food pantry once a year because that's what I'm supposed to do and that's what looks good.

But at the end of the day, every single day are you getting better at helping somebody else getting better and that's what we do with the Driven Foundation and that's what I kind of stand for, what I started.

Because I know what I needed growing up and being in the trenches with these families on day to day basis, I know what they need. I know that we have the resources in Columbus, Ohio, Central Ohio to get it done if we make it a priority.
*"Buckeyes for Life"*

## ROY HALL

- Ohio State Football 2001-2005
- 2002 National Championship
- 2002 Fiesta Bowl
- 2003 Fiesta Bowl
- 2004 Alamo Bowl
- 2005 Fiesta Bowl
- Indianapolis Colts – 2007-2009
- New Orleans Saints – 2010
- Detroit Lions – 2010

*A very recent "Buckeye for Life" Jay Richardson Pays Forward in a very big way!*

We have an incredible "Buckeye Brotherhood" at Ohio State among all our former teammates and players. Our teammates are our brothers. While I was in the NFL with the Oakland Raiders, my teammates were co-workers.

Paying Forward and philanthropic efforts were emphasized at Ohio State, especially after football, but my mother, Deborah Johnson, also got me involved.

"How you're perceived is sometimes more important than how you are," Richardson said. "My mother always taught me to stay on the right path and stay focused. She taught me to always look someone in the eye when you're talking to them and to treat people the right way.

"Me and my mother started this foundation back in 2009. I was coming off my second year in the NFL and it was basically, my mom pulling me aside and saying, 'Listen, I know you're very, very focused on what you're doing in the NFL and I know it requires a great deal of your focus, but in the offseason, we really need to focus on what our give back is going to be and how you want to "Pay Forward" to Columbus.' I was like, 'You know what? You're right. I've been just locked into this, but let's do it.'

"Literally, we just sat down and said, 'All right, here's what we're going to do.' All my buddies were having football camps, so, we thought the best thing to do was to do a life skills camp. Let's do a camp that teaches a lot of these kids how to navigate through life and how to really be effective and to teach them how to pick their focus post-high school. Let's teach them a set of skills that helps them navigate through not just college, but also, possibly, the job market.' That's what the Jay Richardson Foundation eventually evolved into. Our very first life skills camp was far simpler than that.

"I mean, we literally—we're bringing the kids in to learn just basic skills. A lot of these kids come from single parent homes. Most of these kids didn't have fathers in their life. My biological father wasn't in my life in a lot of my younger years and in high school so I can sympathize with that. I wanted to let these kids know that I get what you've been through and there's still tons of ways you could be successful, but there's a lot of things you don't know so, let's take it from the top with simple stuff.

"Literally, our very first camp, I'll never forget, we were teaching kids how to tie a tie, how to fill out a checkbook, how to apply for something online, just the basics, just the stuff that no one tells you or the kind of thing that you would learn from a father figure or a parent at home. I think a lot of kids really didn't have that. It was pretty cool for them to see how much of an interest we took in their success.

"As we evolved, we decided, here's what some of these families really need. It became a career building camp. Every year, we have a couple career building camps for the kids. When I said career building, we bring in people from all walks of life: doctors, lawyers, people at the police department, firefighters, almost every profession that should be represented.

"We sit them all down into a big room with all these career leaders. The kids will get the chance to spend some time one-on-one with every job in there, talk to them about just what their profession entails, and if they do see themselves doing that one day, how do they go about getting to that level; what coursework should they be taking in college to prepare them for that.

"The goal, ultimately, is how to prepare these kids for the next level of their lives. That's not always college. Me and my mother recognized early on, college is expensive. If you don't have a plan heading into college, you're going to waste thousands of dollars on an education that's not prepared you for anything that you want to do. Many kids who can't afford that—to build a skillset and prepare themselves for the job market. I think having a trade is as valuable.

"My mom had the idea in 2014, 'Listen, we're giving these kids great information and it's going well. We do all of this encouraging and building up in our team summits and foundation events and then what happens? The kids perform, the message is not reinforced by the parents, and ultimately the kids go home upset because their parents aren't with them on this.'

"If the messages are not reinforced then they fall on deaf ears at home and the kids are not supported. We thought maybe we should involve the parents. We really needed to get families, as a whole, involved with what we're doing. That was when things really got cool.

"My mother raised three boys, all of which graduated from college. Two of us had full athletic scholarships and one of us played professionally, myself. Parents will listen to my mother. They'll take her advice to heart because they know she's lived it and that she's successfully raised some boys who did well. I thought that was very important because now we have a way to reach the parents and not just the kids. I'm good with the kids because kids love an athlete and they dream about being able to have those experiences and hear from someone who did something that they want to do one day.

"Parents are different. Parents really connect with my mother because she's lived her life as a single mom and the tough role of raising kids. She can just relate on every level to what these parents are going through. That was critical. So, our foundation direction went from being all about just the kids, and now being about families. How do we help bring together families, how do we help parents get their kids recruited?

"My mom has a whole workshop that she does through Ohio State called the Gifted Athletes, where she literally brings in all of these high school kids who are all potential D1 athletes in a number of different sports. She guides the parents through the recruiting process which is really cool because a lot of parents don't understand it. There's a whole art to understanding recruiting and understanding how to get your kid noticed at the next level."

## Jay Richardson

- Ohio State Football Defensive End 2002 – 2006
- Ohio State Football starting Defensive End – 2006
- Oakland Raiders (2007-2009)
- Seattle Seahawks (2010)
- New York Jets (2012)
- New Orleans Saints (2013)

**Lebron James is a "Self-Proclaimed Buckeye".**

James played high school basketball at St. Vincent–St. Mary High School in his hometown of Akron, Ohio, where he was highly promoted in the national media as a future NBA superstar. After graduating, he was weighing accepting a scholarship offer from The Ohio State University to play both basketball and football, but he was selected by his home team, the Cleveland Cavaliers, as the first overall pick of the 2003 NBA draft.

While Lebron is a World Class Basketball Player, he has an honorary locker in the Ohio State Men's Basketball Locker room, and he is very dedicated and supportive of Ohio State Football.

Lebron comes back to Columbus for the biggest, most important home football game each year and hangs on the sidelines with the team. On more than one occasion, he has walked to the Stadium with the team and given a pep talk to the fans and the Ohio State University Marching band at the "Skull Session" in St. John Arena prior to the games. In his talks to the crowd, he has said, "If I hadn't gone to the NBA and the Cleveland Cavaliers, I would have been right here, wearing scarlet and gray as a Buckeye. I'm a Buckeye for Life," LeBron said. Lebron has also been on the sidelines, supporting the Buckeyes at many of their bowl games, including the 2015 National Championship in Dallas.

Lebron James is also a huge advocate for "Paying Forward," He created the Lebron James Family Foundation in 2005. Since 2005, the foundation has held an annual bike-a-thon in Akron to raise money for various causes.] In 2015, James announced a partnership with the University of Akron to provide scholarships for as many as 2,300 children. Within the Lebron James Family Foundation, he has created the "I Promise Program" which rewards elementary and second education students for their achievements. The kids promise to do the following: TO GO TO SCHOOL. TO DO ALL OF MY HOMEWORK. TO LISTEN TO MY TEACHERS BECAUSE THEY WILL HELP ME LEARN. TO ASK QUESTIONS AND FIND ANSWERS. TO NEVER GIVE UP, NO MATTER WHAT. TO ALWAYS TRY MY BEST. TO BE HELPFUL AND RESPECTFUL TO OTHERS. TO LIVE A HEALTHY LIFE BY EATING RIGHT AND BEING ACTIVE. TO MAKE GOOD CHOICES FOR MYSELF. TO HAVE FUN. AND ABOVE ALL ELSE, TO FINISH SCHOOL!

It is estimated that the LBFF has donated in excess of $45,000,000 to the Akron, Ohio community. That's Paying forward and a definite **Buckeye for Life!**

## LeBron James

- Buckeye for Life
- 2× Mr. Basketball USA – 2002, 2003
- Naismith Prep Player of the Year – 2003
- McDonald's All-American Game – MVP 2003
- 3× Ohio Mr. Basketball – 2001-2003
- Cleveland Cavaliers – 2003-2010
- Miami Heat – 2010-2014
- Cleveland Cavaliers – 2014-present
- 3× NBA champion – 2012, 2013, 2016
- 3× NBA Finals MVP – 2012, 2013, 2016
- 4× NBA MVP – 2009, 10, 12, 13
- 13× NBA All-Star – 2005-2017
- 2× NBA All-Star Game MVP – 2006, 2008
- 11× All-NBA First Team – 2006, 2008-2017
- 2× All-NBA Second Team – 2005, 2007
- 5× NBA All-Defensive First Team – 2009-2013
- NBA Rookie of the Year – 2004
- NBA scoring champion – 2008
- 2× AP Athlete of the Year – 2013, 2016
- 2× *Sports Illustrated* Sportsperson of the Year
  - 2012, 2016
- USA Basketball Male Athlete of the Year – 2012

# 4
# EDUCATION AND DEVELOPMENT

### (Life during and after Football)

Wayne Woodrow Hayes grew up in a family where education was prevalent in everything they did, given that his father, Wayne B. Hayes, was the school superintendent of Newcomerstown High School. It is no wonder that Woody went on to earn his two bachelor's degrees in English and History from Denison University and his Master's degree in Education from The Ohio State University, but more importantly, he became an academic professor and a "life professor," molding and positively influencing thousands of lives along the way.

Coach Hayes created an environment within Ohio State Football that emphasized education and the nature of being a true scholar athlete. During the 1970s, University Admissions were not nearly a selective as they are today. They used to admit nearly 60,000 students and had early basic education classes for the incoming freshmen and sophomores as well that were designed to "thin the herd." Many called them "flunk out" courses. I can still remember some of them today, English 110, History 150.01, and Botany/Zoology 150.02. Woody used to hold classes at 7:00 a.m. each day to prepare his young players to succeed in English 110. While he taught grammar and composition, he led with vocabulary, which he felt was extremely important to passing English 110. He taught the class with a book called "Word Power Made Easy" by Norman Lewis, of which he gave a copy to each player. I passed English 110 and still have that book today. We also had a strict regimen, where members of Larry Romanoff's staff were assigned to ensure we made it to class. After classes, football practice, team meetings, and training table, we were required to attend Study Table from 7:00 to 9:00 p.m. each evening. We were expected to study and complete our assignments and were even provided tutors to ensure we were grasping and learning the materials. We were not allowed to be at Ohio State just for football. That certainly can be attributed to Woody Hayes, but exists in the same way today in 2018 for Buckeye Athletes.

**Woody teaching "Word Power Made Easy"**

***Ohio State Athletics Director, Gene Smith shares his opinions on the education and development environment at Ohio State:"***

"We've been blessed to have good coaches and you think about those coaches and how they tried to not just help our athletes be the best athletes, they tried to help them grow as people. When you focus on the person and you help them grow as a person, usually you're able to have an impact on them where there's some emotional tie.

"I think Woody Hayes, he did that exceptionally well, of course, with helping guys become men. When you're doing that together, if he's doing it for all of them and you're doing it together, the emotions come out. You create this emotional bond with who you're playing with. Tressel was good at that. I watched Urban and what he does with that and then I just watched a video this morning where Curtis Grant at halftime of the National Championship Game was giving a speech to the team, he was all fired up and he says, 'When it gets tough, look to your left, look to your right, look to your brother and give everything you have for your brother.' He was giving an emotional speech at halftime with his teammates. He was a team captain and he was trying to get them inspired to be the best that they can be for the second half and go out and win the championship. That's what he's talking about, is the emotion that goes beyond the technique in the game, it goes beyond how you're lining up, or your first step, or your reads, or any of that thing, is that emotional bond, that comradery that carries over.

"We had unbelievable talent, but it was that comradery among the athletes and the chemistry that was just phenomenal. I see it in all of our sports, our two-time national champions in men's volleyball and they won it back to back. Those kids were tight, you couldn't find a gap in their relationships. It certainly is that way in football, and football has set a standard for that here.

"That's why that happens here constantly. It's part of our culture at Ohio State. Urban operates that way today. All of our assistants operate that way today. For us in our athletic department with 36 sports. All of our coaches operate that way. We have what we call a total student-athlete development program. It's focused around building the individual, building the person. Then building the athlete. Then, helping them grow as people four or five years while they're with us.

"So, when you teach people the value of relationships, respect, and they get it, they're going to be better off. That happens among teammates. That happens when they go to class. So, when they leave here and they go to work, they've got it. What you experienced Tom, every athlete experienced it in a different way. They may not ever get hurt, but they had that connection with Woody, or Dick Walker, or Bill Miles, or whoever. That care created what you talk about, what you're writing about. That created more than the games themselves. That's why we have a lot of Buckeyes move back to Columbus. We have that in every sport, obviously football. A lot of them, guys moving back here who didn't grow up here. Yes, they're building homes, and getting jobs, buying auto dealerships. They connected to this place so much because of the Buckeye Brotherhood."

***Smith explains further:*** "We have that development philosophy in every sport. We require every freshman that comes in, for example, to have a bank account and as you can imagine, many of them don't have bank accounts. We require them to have bank accounts, and then we have a mandatory financial literacy program, where they all learn how to manage money. Then in their sophomore year, they're required to have a resume edited, proofed, and ready to go. Then between their sophomore and during their junior years, we send them to mock interviews. We have a person specifically designed to make sure that they're positioned to get a job when they leave. We track every senior, every junior to be senior on what they're going to do when they're done, because as you well know, a lot of them aren't going pro. I want to know for those who are going to graduate in December, that all of them have a job before they walk out.

"The same thing with the spring athlete graduates. I want every single one of them to have a job before they walk out. We had 214 graduates between December and spring, and only 19 of them didn't have jobs. All the rest of them were going to grad school. There were some that were going to take a year off, but all the rest of them had jobs, or they went pro, some went pro. What we're doing now is tracking those others to make sure that we're giving them all the resources to help them find a job.

"That's the Buckeye way. What you're talking about, that's the Buckeye way. Every sport does not have a Real Life Wednesday, but they have something similar where they bring in people like you, or people that can relate to their culture. People you bring in for football, you don't generally bring in for men's tennis. We do a lot of that programming for our athletes. It's just focusing on the person, helping develop the person."

## Gene Smith

- Notre Dame – Player – 1973 AP National Championship
- Notre Dame – Assistant Coach – 1977 National Championship
- Eastern Michigan University – Athletics Director – 1986-1993
- Iowa State University – Athletics Director – 1993-2000
- Arizona State University – Athletics Director – 2000-2005
- The Ohio State University – Athletics Director – 2005-Present

***Brian Baschangel, after playing four great years for the Ohio State Buckeyes, went on to play 10 years with the Chicago Bears.***

"I had just been drafted in the 2nd round by the Bears," Baschnagel said. "I was feeling pretty good about myself and thought it was time to go pay a visit to coach Hayes. I walked into Woody's office and he immediately asked me, 'What are you going to do?' I wasn't sure exactly what he was asking, so I asked coach Hayes to clarify what he was asking, when again, he said, 'What the hell are you going to do?' I said, 'Well, coach, I was just drafted by the Chicago Bears and I intend to go to Chicago and try and make that team.'

Woody then grabbed a book off his credenza, threw it on the floor and said 'There goes your law degree straight to hell. You're going to go to Chicago, make that team and play for ten years and you'll never come back to Ohio State to finish that law degree.' What a prognosticator Woody was."

Each time he came back to see Coach Hayes, Woody would not let him in the office to talk, until he was finally convinced that Brian was enrolled back at TOSU and progressing toward a degree.

Brian did play for the Bears for 10 years and he did come back to Ohio State to finish his degree, albeit in business, but it was still a great degree from a great university.

It was a great testimonial to Woody's commitment to education, but a parallel commitment by Brian Baschnagel to finish his degree as well. **Buckeyes for Life!**

## Brian Baschnagel

- Ohio State Football 1972-1975
- Ohio State Starting Wingback 1973, 74, 75
- Ohio State – Played in four Rose Bowls
- Academic All-American – 1974, 1975
- National Football Foundation and Hall of Fame scholarship award – 1975
- Chicago Bears 1976-1985

**Rex Kern is one of the all-time great Ohio State football players, who quarterbacked the Buckeyes during the 1968, 1970 and 1971 seasons.**

He was team captain and All-American quarterback of the 1968 National Championship team. The Buckeyes were 27-2 during Kern's tenure and defeated the O.J. Simpson led USC Trojans in the 1969 Rose Bowl. Comparable to a true "Cinderella story," Rex met his wife Nancy at *that* Rose Bowl. Nancy was a Rose Bowl princess who intended to enter USC the following fall. However, after the Kern-led Buckeyes beat the Trojans, he persuaded her to enroll at Ohio State, and they married five years later.

Rex went on and played four years in the National Football League and then returned to Ohio State, where he has proudly earned three academic degrees, his Bachelor of Arts, Masters and Doctorate of Philosophy. "Ohio State has always cared about the education of their players and they really paid that extra attention to us as freshmen to ensure we established a good foundation during our first year.," Kern said. "Woody said to all of us, 'You're going to get a great education at the Ohio State University and it is my responsibility to see that you do.' "When the 'Old Man' took that on, you knew that we should go to class, we would show up on time, we would sit in the front row, and we would set our watches on 'Woody time', ten minutes fast, because you knew the 'old man' set his watch ten minutes fast and we had to do those types of things. Woody had systems in place, through our assistant coaches, so that he knew when we had quizzes, he knew when we had mid-terms, he knew when we had tests, and he made sure we were prepared and he made sure we got it done," Kern said.

"Ohio State has always had a great record on their graduation rate. After I was done and I was working on my Masters and my PHD, I did a longitudinal study on Woody's first 25 years on the graduation rate. Of the Varsity "O" players that played for Woody, he graduated roughly 87.6 percent of its players and *of* those players another 37 percent went on to graduate school. I don't know that any college or university other than the true academic institutions that can boast that and I don't think anybody can come close to that today."

## Rex Kern

- Ohio State Football 1967-1970
- Ohio State Starting Quarterback 1968, 1969, 1979

- 1968 National Championship
- Rose Bowl MVP – 1969
- Baltimore Colts – 1971-1973
- Buffalo Bills – 1974

**Larry Romanoff was the Head Academic Advisor for Football during most of our years at Ohio State.**

I personally believe that Larry Romanoff is one of the greatest Buckeyes ever, regardless of the fact that his countless efforts were most often accomplished behind the scenes or under the radar. Amazingly, each and every one of the former players that I have spoken with have said the very same thing. We will never forget all the great things that Larry has done for us.

As I entered Ohio State as a freshman, I was enamored by our great university, but I was also full of myself, thinking that I was "bigger than life," now playing for one of the greatest powers in college football. I felt things should be given to me or certainly made easier, including classes and my grades. Oh, how wrong I was! During my freshman year, I had missed classes and failed to apply myself to my studies, believing that things would be handed to me.

One day, on the way to the then Ernie Biggs Athletic Facility for practice, I was summoned to Larry's office at St. John arena. I knew something was up. When I walked in to Larry's office, there sat my father, who had been notified by Larry Romanoff that I was under performing in my school work. My dad had taken a day off from his engineering position at the Caterpillar Tractor Company to drive nine hours to visit with Larry and to help set his son straight. I was told that I would not be allowed to attend the Gator Bowl with the team unless my grades improved dramatically. To put it mildly, I studied my butt off! I was not going to let them down, but I also learned not to let myself down. It was a pivotal moment in my experience at Ohio State. It taught me how to be a Buckeye, that nothing comes easy and you have to earn everything you get. It was one of those parental moments, not only with my father, but with Larry as well. Needless to say, but my grades improved substantially and I participated in that Gator Bowl and the Rose Bowl the following year.

## LARRY ROMANOFF

- Ohio State Football Team Manager 1969
- Assistant Academic Advisor for the football team
- Head Academic Adviser
- Assistant Athletics Director for Academics
- Director of Development
- Director of External Relations.

# BUCKEYES FOR LIFE

## THE OHIO STATE UNIVERSITY RANKED NO.1 IN THE NATION FOR FOOTBALL AND EDUCATION

By Nick Clarkson on July 9, 2017 at 10:41 am @realsilvertuna_

"We ain't come to play school" no more.

The Ohio State University was ranked No. 1 for the nation's best school to play football and get an education, according an article from USA Today College.

The Buckeyes topped the list above schools such as Notre Dame, Alabama, Wisconsin and USC. The ranking system is based on a number of factors, including athletic competitiveness and overall college quality.

Urban Meyer took notice of the article, and was a fan.

# TOM LEVENICK

**Urban Meyer**
@OSUCoachMeyer

The Ohio State University - #1 for great football AND education! No place like it!!! college.usatoday.com/2017/07/07/bes...

8:58 AM - 9 Jul 2017

**Play Division 1 football and get a great education at these 10 sch...**
The colleges are ranked by the success of the specific sports team as well as the academic progress of the athletes.

college.usatoday.com

**BUCKEYE ACADEMICS**

TERRY McLAURIN · WR · '83
2017 AUTUMN GRADUATE

**2.86**

2017 CUMULATIVE
TEAM GPA

# 5

# 'WE REMEMBER WOODY"

## (Tapping the memories of former Buckeye players)

Wayne Woodrow Woody Hayes became the epitome and leading icon for Ohio State Football. He did so because of so many personal traits of character, integrity, education, work ethic, and devotion to the state of Ohio and The Ohio State University. What I have learned over the years was that Woody made EVERYONE feel appreciated and valued. Being cared for and feeling important builds confidence. Confidence builds success and in Woody's life success meant victories for the Buckeyes. That lesson of caring and building confidence allowed me to be the best leader that I could be, once I entered the business world.

While I have been writing this book, I have had the pleasure visiting with many former players and coaches that have played and coached for Woody Hayes. One element that has been a common denominator is that all of them feel that Woody was the greatest influence on their lives or the second greatest, behind their fathers.

Woody positively impacted our lives in so many ways. All of these former players and coaches, including myself, are now in their 50's, 60's, and 70's and have related to me that they all have "life lessons" which they learned from Woody and they continue to apply them to their lives and daily routines to this very day. There are not enough pages to begin to cover the thousands of lessons Coach Hayes taught, but let's look at a few.

### *The great Archie Griffin shares his feelings about Woody Hayes:*

"Woody, he had that type of impact on people, because I tell people to this day that there is not a day that goes by that I don't think about Woody Hayes. There is not one day that goes by that I don't think about Woody Hayes in some sort of way. Either somebody will remind me of something that he may have said or I would see something happen that would remind me of something that he might have said. As I look at what's going on politically here and I see how Donald Trump is battling the media, I'll never forget those words of what Woody said, 'Don't do battle with those who buy the ink by the barrel because you can never win,' and I think of that because when stuff comes up like that, it reminds me of Woody, every day.

"It was just amazing, the impact that he had on those of us who had the opportunity to play for him because not only was he a great, great coach but he was a wise, wise man and that's what I liked most about him because he was always there for you as you mentioned in your story, he was always there for you. He'll do whatever he can to help you. I mean, he was that type of person, unbelievable. We were very, very fortunate to have that opportunity to play for him and have him be a part of our lives. I know the person I think about every day is my father and Woody was quite like him in the sense that he had that sort of impact for me to think about him every day. He will always be somebody that will be a part of my life.

"When we were playing Michigan one year in Ann Arbor, it would have been 1975, and I think Woody felt that the team was kind of tight and we're having our pregame meal and a lot of pretty young ladies were serving us and Woody thought they were Michigan students and Woody went into the kitchen and he told the guys who were cooking the food to come into the room and serve us because Bo Schembechler planted those pretty girls there to distract us and make sure that we're distracted before we play the University of Michigan. That one was funny because everybody just broke up laughing when he told us that, so I will never forget that and I think he did that for a reason.

"I think he felt that we were tight and we needed to loosen up a little bit and to me that was a ploy that he used to loosen us up a little bit so that we wouldn't be so tight because he always talked about you can't be too tight going into a game. If you're too tight, you're just not going to be able to do the things that you want to do. You got to loosen up a little bit and I think that was a way he had of helping us loosen up because we all broke out laughing and you could see him crack a little smile when he said that to the team. Bo planted them here to distract us."

**Former Buckeye Assistant Coach and Hall of Fame Notre Dame Head Coach Lou Holtz remembers Woody:**

"There are just so many memories of Coach Hayes. Everybody talked about how tough he was and how demanding, and that's absolutely true. He just believed in being the best you can be.

"So, we beat the number one team in the country, the game's over like at 4:35, we had staff meetings at seven o'clock that night, watching film for our next game against Northwestern and getting ready for the next week.

"You couldn't even celebrate it, but that was just Coach Hayes.

Coach Hayes had a huge devotion to his players, he just—you couldn't say enough good things about him, the things I learned from him, that type of person he was. We also had a great staff. Almost everybody went on to become a head coach. Hugh Hindman became AD at Ohio State, Lou McCullough became AD at Iowa State, Bill Mallory became head coach at Colorado and Indiana. Earl Bruce became head coach at Iowa State and Ohio State, Ruddy Hubbard became head coach at Florida A&M, George Chaump became head coach at the Naval Academy, Dave McClain who replaced Bill became head coach at Wisconsin. Let's see I think that—I think that covers all the staff except those who had no desire to be a head coach.

"Everybody else went on to become head coaches after that, but the loyalty you have until the last day, it remains even to this day, absolutely."

## Lou Holtz

- Iowa Assistant – 1960
- William and Mary Assistant – 1961-1963
- Connecticut Assistant – 1964-1965
- South Carolina Assistant – 1966-1967
- Ohio State Assistant – 1968
- Ohio State National Champion – 1968
- William and Mary Head Coach – 1969-1971
- NC State Head Coach – 1972-1975
- New York Jets Head Coach – 1976
- Arkansas Head Coach – 1977-1983

- Minnesota Head Coach – 1984-1985
- Notre Dame Head Coach – 1986-19964
- Notre Dame National Championship – 1988
- South Carolina Head Coach – 1999-2004
- College Football Hall of Fame – 2008
- ESPN College Football Analyst – 2008-present

**Cornelius Green had some unique memories of Coach Woody Hayes:**

"Whenever you're a quarterback at Ohio State, you're probably going to spend more time with Woody than any other position player. Mine wasn't one of the greatest stories, but Woody had me sick all the time and of course, I couldn't sleep at night and so I had to go see Dr. Murphy, who was our team doctor at the time. Dr. Bob told me I was number five and I thought he was joking because my number was seven and he said that I was the fifth quarterback Woody had given an ulcer to.

"So, Woody had given ulcers to Rex Kern and Tom Matte and I can't think of the other two that he had given an ulcer prior to me. Football was everything, but of course, football was a big business as well. One of my great Woody stories was for him giving me an ulcer in addition to making me a great quarterback by putting pressure on me every day and practice. The kind of pressure that playing in front of 100,000 people creates. So, that's the kind of pressure Woody put on you ever day to be great. I guess that kind of summarizes two good stories in terms of what Ohio State means to me, what it means to be a teammate, and what a coach is meant to be."

***Doug Donley shares his thoughts on Wood Hayes:***

"I remember Woody telling us something that I use today when I coach all my kid's teams and that is 'The problem with youth today is that they're better than they think they are. They just don't believe in themselves.' He always preached that. 'They're better than they think they are. You need to wear them down and build them up.' I always thought that was amazing, so I made up some t-shirts for my kid's teams, imprinted with the letters, B.A.M., which stands for **B**elieve in yourself, **A**ttitude, and **M**ental Toughness. Kids doubt themselves and they don't understand how good they are or how good they can be. Woody was the master of building confidence and it's just amazing when you think back on all the things that Woody taught us and how true they are. It's really something."

### *Stan White reveals his memories:*

"I can remember Woody talking constantly about dedication and not missing practice, no matter what. On cold rainy days, he used to say, 'If you're going to fight in the Atlantic, you've got to train in the Atlantic.' You know, there isn't a day that goes by, that I don't think of Woody or apply one of his teachings and I think it was just yesterday when one of our entry level employees came to me and said that he was going to take a day off of training and I said to him, my old coach used to tell me that 'If you miss one day of practice YOU know it, if you miss two days of practice, YOUR CRITICS will know it and if you miss three days of practice, EVERYBODY will know it.' You know, life teaches you how right those sayings were that he used and there isn't a day that goes by that I don't think about him some way; something that he said or a funny story or an axiom that he left me with for the rest of my life that proved so true. He was just a great man and an inspiration to everybody that ever played for him. Not everybody liked him, while they played for him, but I don't know of anybody that doesn't revere him and like him for the experiences he gave them that last a lifetime."

## Stan White

- *Ohio State Linebacker and Kicker – 1969-1971*
- *Buckeye Team Captain 1971*
- *Detroit Lions linebacker 1972-1981*

**Prior to passing, former Ohio State Head Coach Earle Bruce shared a memory from his years as a Buckeye Coach:**

"It is my first year as an assistant and we are in the middle of spring practice and I didn't feel well after practice. So, I went in to see Ernie Biggs (Head Trainer) and Dr. Bob Murphy. They said, 'What's the problem?' And I say, 'You know, I'm feeling rather tight around the chest.' And they said, 'Tightness of the chest?' And then they started to laugh. And I said, 'What's so funny?' And they said, 'Join the club.' I said, 'What club am I joining?' Dr. Bob said, 'Every first-year assistant football coach that's ever coached here for Coach Hayes has come in here and said they have tightness around the chest.' I said, 'Well, what do you do about it?' Dr. Bob said, 'This is what you do about it. Do you see this?' I said 'Yeah, what is it?' He said, 'Its valium. I'm going to give you a prescription for this and I want you to go home, take one of these, fill up your bathroom tub with 12 to 14 inches of hot water, lock the door, get in the tub and cuss Coach Hayes out for about a 45-minute period and you'll feel a hell of a lot better.' So,

I go home and I'm telling my wife Jeanne what they told me to do and she said, 'Are you really going to do that?' And I said' That's what they told me to do.'

"So, I get in the tub and I started cussing out Coach Hayes and forget about my two daughters, who are ages four and two. They're outside the bathroom and start yelling 'Who's in there with Daddy, Mommy? Who's in there with Daddy, Mommy?' So, Jeanne had to take them outside, because Daddy was cussing out Woody Hayes. I thought, what the hell is a grown man doing in the bathtub doing that? Coach Hayes really affected you a little differently. There are many guys that could only coach one year under Coach Hayes, but if you could stick out six, you deserved about two medals, I guess. I'll tell you what I'm proud of is that I was an assistant coach to Coach Hayes for six years. I coached the offensive line and the defensive backs. That's a long time at Ohio State to be an assistant to Coach Hayes. I learned a lot and came out of it a better man, tougher than you would normally be."

## **EARLE BRUCE**

- Ohio State University Graduate – 1953
- Ohio State Football Assistant Coach – 1966-1971
- Tampa University Head Coach – 1972
- Iowa State Head Coach – 1973-1978
- Ohio State Head Coach – 1979-1987
- College Football Hall of Fame – Inducted 2002

**One of the true Icons of the Woody Hayes era at Ohio State, was none other than Harold "Champ" Henson.**

Champ epitomized "three yards and a cloud of dust", the "Robust T" and the "Power I," which were all trademarks of Woody Hayes and The Ohio State Buckeyes." Henson played fullback for the Buckeyes from 1972-1974 and led the Nation in scoring as a sophomore in 1972. Knee injuries hampered his ability to play his junior and senior seasons, but he was still drafted by the Minnesota Vikings in 1975 and then played one year for the Cincinnati Bengals, before returning to his roots in farming and managing Henson's Farms in Ashville Ohio.

Champ jumped right in with his thoughts and perspectives on Woody. "The Old Man's personality represented such a broad spectrum from the most worthless tyrant to the most benevolent grandfather and you might get them both the same day!" Henson said laughing. "When I started at OSU, being the Ohio State Fullback was like being the fullback of America. The Ohio State offense revolved around the fullback position until Archie came in and then there was a transition to the tailback," he said. "You know, being the fullback and being next to Woody on every play in practice was really intense."

"So, I go through my freshman year, which was the last year when freshmen were ineligible to play, and Woody is on me like a wet pair of shorts," Henson said. "I progress into my sophomore year and I am the low man on the totem pole. I am the whipping boy. I'm the one getting kicked in the butt and I'm the one getting the left hooks to the solar plexus when I made a mistake. But, I keep working and working and I finally move up to number two on the depth chart."

"Now, it's the Thursday night before the first game against Iowa and Woody comes in to my room and tells me he wants to talk for a minute," Henson tells me while choking back tears. "Then, he tells me 'Champ, you've worked really hard and I've been really tough on you, but now it is all coming together.' He said, 'Saturday, you're going to play a lot, and I expect you to be at your very best. Now, why don't you call and tell your mom and dad.' Woody said, 'I think they'll get a big kick out of it.'

"The next day on the very first play of the game I fumble the ball on our own 20-yard line on my very first carry in Ohio Stadium. The very next play, either Randy Gradishar or Rick Middleton forces a fumble and we are going back the other way. So, before Woody can rip my ass, I'm back on the field in the huddle, and do you know Woody came back with the very same play. I run for 14 yards and a first down and the rest is history. I ran for two touchdowns and we beat Iowa 21 - 0.

You know," Henson said, "there was a method to his madness, although I'm still figuring some of it out today after all these years. On the other end of the spectrum that I mentioned earlier, I remember a story from my senior year. It was during two-a-days, sometime between training table and meetings, when Woody pulled me aside and said, 'Champ, I just talked to your dad, and your mom has been admitted to Grant Hospital.' He said, 'you don't need to be in these meetings or practice, you know this stuff as good as anybody. You need to go and see your mom.' Then he said, 'Here, take my car' (handing Champ the keys to his Ranchero pickup truck.) Then Woody said, 'My truck needs gas,' and he gave me a twenty-dollar bill. He said, 'put gas in my truck and oh, by the way, there's a nice little gift shop in the hospital, make sure you get something nice for your mom.'

"So, I go to put gas in Woody's truck and the tank is totally full. That was just his way of slipping me twenty dollars so I could get something for my mom," Henson said. "So, I go see my mom and it's nothing life threatening, but she is going to need to be in the hospital for four to five days. I then go back to and explain the situation to Woody and I hand him the twenty-dollar bill and tell him his truck didn't need any gas. 'Yes, it did!' Woody said curtly. I said, 'No coach, the tank was full!' Woody said, 'You're wrong,' and turned and walked away."

Now, as Champ is telling me this, he is trying to choke back the tears again. "The next morning at 7:00 a.m., Anne Hayes (Woody's wife) showed up at our family farm and my dad says, 'Anne, what are you doing here?' To which she replied, 'You can't run a farm without a woman and I'm here to help.' My dad politely says, 'Anne, we don't really need any help, we'll get by,' when Anne, a chip off Woody's block interrupts him and says, 'You damned fool, get out of the way and what do you want for breakfast?' That was typical Anne Hayes," said Henson. "So, she stayed for three days and made sure they were fed and that my brothers got off to school on time. You know, we lived 30 miles away from Columbus and that was a story I'll never forget," Champ said gaining his composure.

"These were the types of things that Woody did all the time for people that the public never saw," Henson said. "And quite frankly, he didn't want people to see them. It was always about paying forward, never about paying any attention to him, what so ever." **Buckeyes for Life!**

## HAROLD "CHAMP" HENSON

- *Ohio State Fullback 1972-1974*
- *1972 NCAA Touchdown Leader – 20*
- *1972 NCAA Rushing Touchdown Leader – 20*
- *1972 NCAA Scoring Leader – 120 points*

### *Ernie Andria has some great* **Woody** *Stories:*

"When we were at the Sugar Bowl in 1977 and we're in a meeting room in a hotel, and Woody is giving us this big-time speech about Alabama. But his false teeth - I never knew Woody had false teeth, and you have to hear this story. He kept talking and them gosh darn front teeth kept falling out of this mouth, and he shoved them back up into his mouth about, I don't know, five or six times. And then finally he just says, 'Oh, God damn son of a bitch.' He pulled his freaking teeth out, and he had them in his hand, and he's just barking at us with no front teeth. It was the funniest damn thing I've ever seen in my life. It was just hilarious, just hilarious. That was just crazy.

Another Story I remember—I guess the birthday party over at the Drake Union. The birthday party with me and Woody and Anne Hayes, all the recruits and my parents. That was very memorable for me because we had a big birthday cake that said, 'Happy Birthday Ernie Andria and Woody Hayes.' And they cut that cake in half that had that on it and gave it to me. And my mother-in-law had that cake in her freezer for probably 20, 25 years. I never saw it after that. She called me one day and said, 'Ern, my freezer broke. What would you like me to do with this cake?' And I said, 'Oh, just throw it away.' That was pretty memorable for me because I guess I just didn't realize that our birthdays were on the same day at that point. We're both left handed, and we're both jelly bellied. And from that day on it was like he just always had a little thing for me, and It was nice. My parents were just on cloud nine. And Woody, he took a liking to me. They call me little Woody. You knew that right?"

## Ernie Andria

- Ohio State Football 1976-1979
- Starting Left Guard – 1979
- 1977 Sugar Bowl
- 1978 Gator Bowl
- 1980 Rose Bowl

**Tom Skladany had some humorous memories of Woody:**

"Woody always told us, 'If anyone ever gives you a compliment, kick em in the shins unless it's a lady over 80!' **How would like to hear that from your coach when you are 18 years old!** Skladany said. "When asked, Woody told us that when someone compliments you they are actually hurting you because you lose your edge and start believing your press clippings. He said many times his teams were undefeated and the press started extolling the virtues of the top players, and the next thing you knew a loss came upon them, so in Woody's world ... they were actually hurting you with a compliment so 'kick em in the shins unless it's a lady over 80!'

"Back in 1975, on a bright sunny day in the off season, I was getting ready to leave my apartment to go golfing, and Woody called and asked me if I was going out to punt that afternoon...Woody loved watching punts in the air and often called me to go watch me practice in the off season. I told him that I wasn't and when he asked why I said, 'Coach, I have to give air traffic controllers at Port Columbus International Airport a 12 hour notice before I go punt so they have time to redirect incoming flights'...he said, 'WHAT?'....then after a brief silence he hung up and 4 minutes later I get a call from my kicking coach (Coach Ralph Staub) and he asked me if I was screwing with Woody and I said, 'NO'...and he said, 'Well Woody just called me and told me to keep you away from him.' Stauber cried laughing when I came clean."

## TOM SKLADANY

- *Ohio State Football 1973-1976*
- *Ohio State Starting Punter, Kicker – 1974, 75, 76*
- *Ohio State – All American 1974, 75, 76*
- *The only 3-time first team All American punter in NCAA history*
- *Philadelphia Eagles – 1983*
- *All Pro, 1978-1982 (AP, UPI, Sporting News)*
- *Pro Bowl 1981*
- *Detroit Lions 1978-1982*

Larry Romanoff might have more memories and stories about Woody Hayes than anyone. "I remember one evening after practice and study table when I was team manager," Larry said. "Woody came up to me and said, 'Larry, do you have your homework done?' When I told him yes, that I was all caught up, Woody said, 'Good, I have a football to deliver to a terminal cancer patient in Cleveland and I'd like you to come along.'

"It had been a long day, but we jumped in the car and drove two and a half hours to Mt. Sinai Hospital in Cleveland. We went into the Cancer Ward and Woody delivered an autographed football to this man who was terminal with cancer. He spent 25 to 30 minutes speaking with this gentleman, offering him care and encouragement. You should have seen the look on his face. We then drove back to Columbus and the Biggs Facility, where Woody went right to the film room to watch films of that day's practice.

"Many years later, I met a man here in Columbus, who asked how long I had worked with Ohio State Football. When I told him that I had been there from 1969 to the present, the man said, 'then you must have worked for the great Woody Hayes.' When I told him that I did, he told me the story of how his mother worked in the Neo-Natal department of the Ohio State University Hospital and had told him how Woody used to frequently arrive in the wee hours of the morning to help feed the babies. 'My Mom loved him ever since,' he said."

Regarding that same paying forward topic, I asked Larry to share some of his best memories while at Ohio State. Not surprisingly, Larry said, "One of the greatest experiences was to work with Woody Hayes, Earle Bruce, John Cooper, an awesome person like Jim Tressel and now Urban Meyer." **Buckeyes for Life!**

# 6

# "THE BUCKEYE DYNASTY"

## (The People, The Tradition, The Excellence, The Pride & Passion)

After the 2016 season, the Associated Press ranked the Top 25 College Football programs of all time. The AP has been ranking the best teams in college football since 1936. Over 81 years and 1,119 polls, a total of 167 schools have been ranked and 44 of them have been ranked No. 1. To determine the all-time Top 25, the AP formula counted poll appearances (one point) to mark consistency, No. 1 rankings (two points) to acknowledge elite programs and gave a bonus for AP championships (10 points).

**AP** TOP 100 PROGRAMS OF ALL TIME          **AP Associated Press**

### A.P. Top 25 of All Time
1. Ohio State
2. Oklahoma
3. Notre Dame
4. Alabama
5. USC
6. Nebraska
7. Michigan
8. Texas
9. Florida State
10. Florida
11. LSU
12. Penn State
13. Miami of Florida
14. Tennessee
15. Auburn
16. Georgia
17. UCLA
18. Texas A&M
19. Michigan State
20. Washington
21. Clemson
22. Arkansas
23. Pittsburgh
24. Wisconsin
25. Iowa

While the Associated Press rates Ohio State as the #1 college football program of all time, based on poll appearances and National Championships, I believe it is much more than that.

Yes, we have won eight National Championships, 36 Big Ten Championships, seven Heisman Trophies, six Lombardi

Awards, five Outland Trophies and had 196 First Team All American Players, but there is an equal or possibly even greater amount of quality versus that quantity.

Ohio State has a firm foundation of great people, great traditions, and excellence. We have an incredible, large fan base that is resounding with pride and passion for their Buckeyes. Adding all those elements together results in the most elite program in college football. Pairing that with the "Best Damn Band in the Land" creates a wonderful experience on a crisp fall Saturday in Columbus, Ohio.

**Tom Luginbill, College Football Analyst for ESPN Sports Television offered up his thoughts on the Ohio State Football program.**

"Ohio State, more than any other program in America, has been able to maintain its elite status – not over the years or decades, but over the generations. They have transcended the generations and will continue to do that long after we are gone," Luginbill said. "It is a combination of the victories and championships, the commitment to character and education and the support of a huge fan base and alumni association around the world."

## Tom Luginbill

- ESPN – College Football Analyst
- Palomar JC – Football 1992-1993
- Georgia Tech Football 1994
- Eastern Kentucky Football – 1995

**Chris Spielman shares his thoughts on Ohio State Football.**

"Ohio is a Football State. You have the NFL Hall of Fame. You have the Browns and the Bengals, but Ohio State is Ohio's Football team. It transcends the state.

"In Ohio, everybody is the biggest Buckeye fan and they are not bashful to admit it. When you put all those people together you have a special, special place and Ohio State Football is special.

"As a player, it is a privilege and an honor to play at Ohio State. Ohio State isn't privileged to have you play there. YOU have the privilege to be one of the chosen few who have the God given ability to be a Buckeye Football player." That is where our bond is created.

"I grew up watching Ohio State football," he said. "On Sunday, my brother and I would watch the replays of Youngstown State, the replays of Notre Dame and always the Ohio State replays. My final decision came down to Ohio State and Michigan," Chris said.

"But Bo Schembechler really did a job on me. When I told my dad, he said I'll tell you where you're going you traitor. You're going to Ohio State. It was the best decision I ever made," Spielman said laughing. Spielman then went on to a great career with the Buckeyes and in the NFL. He played in the Rose Bowl, the Citrus Bowl and the Cotton Bowl. He was a two-time All American in 1986 and 1987, won the Lombardi award in 1987, elected to the College Football Hall of Fame and was voted to the NFL Pro Bowl four times.

There have been many great linebackers at TOSU. Names like Stan White, Randy Gradishar, Rick Middleton, Tom Cousineau, Marcus Marek, Chris Spielman, Pepper Johnson, Rowland Tatum, Andy Katzenmoyer, James Laurinaitis and AJ Hawk, just to name a few. I asked Chris who he thought was the best linebacker to ever play at Ohio State. "That's a tough question as there were different circumstances, different offensive styles as well as team mates," Chris said. "But I'll tell you one thing. There's a school about eight hours east of here that calls themselves 'Linebacker U.' That's BS," Chris said, 'The real 'Linebacker U' is right here in Columbus, Ohio."

## Chris Spielman

- *Ohio State Football 1984-1987*
- *Ohio State Starting Linebacker 1984-1987*
- *2× Consensus All-American 1986, 1987*
- *Ohio State Buckeyes MVP – 1987*
- *Lombardi Award – 1987*
- *Chic Harley Award – 1987*
- *Sam B. Nicola Award – 1983*
- *Detroit Lions – 1988-1995*
- *Buffalo Bills – 1996-1997*
- *Cleveland Browns – 1999*
- *4× Pro Bowl – 1989-1991, 1994*
- *3× All-Pro – 1991, 1992, 1994*

**Lou Holtz share his thoughts on the "Buckeye Dynasty:"**

"I was at Ohio State a year and a half before I became a head coach. We won the national championship when I was there and the loyalty that those players have is unparalleled. I'd say this, if there's an individual that has a problem or difficulty, then immediately everybody on that team, including the coaches are notified. Even some people that weren't on that team, like somebody I recruited, like John Hicks.

"He was a great player there's no doubt, but his loyalty to Ohio State was unbelievable. When Jack Tatum was ill, John went to the end of the earth to help him.

"I coached there, I had some great players. Jack Tatum, Tim Anderson, Ted Provost, and Mike Sensibaugh. We had a player named Mike Polaski, who was my fifth back. He went on to become a police fireman. He was injured unbelievably and it was amazing how the whole team rallied around Mike Polaski. It didn't matter whether you're a star or whatever, but the loyalty amongst the team and they had and the fans. The stadium is always filled. Ohio State, it's a very, very special place. I think it's because of their leadership they've had there.

"You go back and Woody Hayes who was there forever. Who absolutely loved that place and developed a love in his players for that place also. Then Earle also did a great job, then Jim Tressel, and then Urban Meyer who I hired at Notre Dame. They just provide great leadership.

"I went up and spoke to the Ohio State Football team a week ago, and I spoke to them for about 40 minutes and I was so impressed with those players. I talked to them a bit about the tradition of Ohio State and everyone sat up in their chair, looked at me the whole time. When I said, 'I've been your age, you've never been mine, I want to share some thoughts and ideas with you.'

"They get out a paper and notebook and take notes. I've never had that any place I've ever been. That describes a special message about Ohio State."

### *Alan Brady shares his thoughts on the Ohio State Experience:*

"You hear guys from other schools talk about their college experience, it wasn't anywhere near what it was at Ohio State," said Alan Brady, President Emeritus of the Varsity "O" Alumni Society.

"Ohio State recruits personal character and athleticism. The extra advantage is all that bonding and the fact everybody sings off the same song sheet. "After you go through four years of blood, sweat, and tears, then you have a few championships that you've reveled in together. That's where I think a lot of the bonding comes from."

## ALAN BRADY

- Ohio State Lacrosse – 1971-1975
- Ohio State Lacrosse Letterman – 1973, 1974, 1975
- Ohio State Lacrosse Team Captain – 1975
- Varsity "O" Alumni Association – President – 2004-2006

**Women's Basketball Great, Katie Smith has some great perspective on "The Buckeye Dynasty" in college athletics:**

"In college, the elite programs, first of all, we at Ohio State have the numbers, we have the largest number of sports programs in the country," Smith said. "There is the ability for us to attract students that are interested in all the sports. I think it's the support, the coaches, the support that you have throughout the university from the academic services, and the great athletic facilities. From the Athletic Director to the President, you have university-wide support.

Part of our culture as a Buckeye is to root for all of our teams. Even the ones that you don't know about. There's so many sports that you don't almost know. Take the Olympics as an example. You might never have heard of the sport before, but when an American's competing, you're cheering with everything you have for that person and vice versa. Just as a Buckeye, when there's success or there's a team competing, ultimately, your heart pulls you in that direction to cheer them on. It's like a brotherhood or sisterhood. I do think it's the attention and the energy that the university puts into not only the athletic department, but the university in general. They want you to succeed. There's a genuine desire and effort, that once you're there, they want you to have the best experience possible.

"It's a support thing, something where they want you to have the ability, the resources, to not only perform your school work but also get the education along with it. There's a lot of things that all come together that just don't exist in a lot of other places. It's really special.

"I do think once you are a part it, it fixes into you. You try to find the best leaders to carry and then you obviously try to share that with the players and let them know just how special this is. I'm sure when they recruit, they try to bring them on campus to just show them what it's like, the energy, just what it looks like. When you think about it, compared to other universities, is just all encompassing, it's everywhere I travel. Everywhere I've gone, whether overseas or other states, you constantly run into somebody who's from the Ohio State and there's just nothing like it.

"I've been on the Buckeye Cruise for Cancer for a few years and I'm like that's insane, the whole cruise ship full of Buckeyes. That's the bond that you have felt with every single person and of course, it's for a great cause to raise money to fight cancer. It's unreal to have that support of those people passionate to give back and to enjoy each other and have a blast for a cause and it's all Buckeyes. Sometimes when you look at it, it's just really unreal, it's like how much we rally around causes or wanted to help."

## KATIE SMITH

- Ohio State Women's Basketball – 1992-1996
- Big Ten Player of the Year (1996)
- Chicago Tribune Silver Basketball (1996)
- Ohio State Athletics Hall of Fame – 2001
- Olympic Gold Medalist – 200, 2004, 2008
- 2× WNBA champion (2006, 2008)
- WNBA Finals MVP (2008)
- 2× All-WNBA First Team (2001, 2003)
- 7× WNBA All-Star (2000-2003, 2005, 2006, 2009)
- WNBA scoring champion (2001)
- WNBA's All-Decade Team (2006)
- WNBA's Top 15 Players of All Time (2011)
- WNBA Top 20@20 (2016)
- All Time Leading Scorer in Women's Professional Basketball
- WNBA New York Liberty Head Coach – 2017-Present

# 7
## "THE RIVALRY"

(The Greatest Rivalry in North American Sports according to ESPN)

1. Ohio State vs Michigan (NCAA Football)
2. Muhammad Ali vs Joe Frazier
3. North Carolina vs Duke (NCAA Basketball)
4. Wilt Chamberlain vs Bill Russel (NBA Basketball)
5. Toronto Maple Leafs vs Montreal Canadiens (NHL)
6. Arnold Palmer vs Jack Nicklaus (PGA Tour)
7. Boston Red Sox vs New York Yankees (MLB)
8. Auburn vs Alabama (NCAA Football)
9. Washington Redskins vs Dallas Cowboys (NFL)
10. San Francisco Giants vs L.A. Dodgers (MLB)

Results from a 2000 poll of the Top 10 Rivalries in the history of North American Sports as conducted by ESPN

The Ohio State/Michigan Game, or "The Game" as it is often called, is considered by many to be the greatest rivalry in North American Sports and certainly the greatest in college football. It has attracted particular national interest over the last four decades as most of the games have determined the Big Ten Conference title and the resulting Rose Bowl match-up, and many have influenced the outcome of the National College Football championship. The game was ranked by ESPN in 2000 as the greatest North American sports rivalry.

The two schools first met in 1897, and the rivalry has been played annually since 1918. The game has been played at the end of the regular season since 1935. Since 1918, the game's site has alternated between Columbus, Ohio, and Ann Arbor, Michigan (Michigan hosts it in odd years and Ohio State in even years) and has been played in Ohio Stadium since 1922 and Michigan Stadium since 1927. Through 2010, Ohio State and Michigan have decided the Big Ten Conference championship between themselves on 22 different occasions and have affected the determination of the conference title an additional 27 times.

**Keith Byars embraces "The Rivalry:"**

"That last Saturday in November, 'Hey, you know we have to beat that team Up North. We have to beat them.' Whether you grew up into it or you were recruited into it the rivalry between us and them, it's always with you no matter what you do, where you go.

"Just this past summer, I was at a golf tournament," Byars said. "And a guy from Michigan, he looked at me and he said something funny to me because he won our flight, but they finished second in the tournament. He said, 'What about that?' I was like, 'Yes but you guys from Michigan, you're used to finishing second.' The whole crowd busted out laughing. 'You're used to that runner up stuff.' It never ends, whether it's in the middle of summer, waiting for football season it's always there, every day of your life."

## Keith Byars

- Ohio State Football 1983-1986
- Ohio State Starting Running Back 1984, 85, 86
- Ohio State Consensus All-American – 1984
- Ohio State – 2$^{nd}$ in voting for the Heisman – 1984
- Philadelphia Eagles – 1986-1992
- Miami Dolphins – 1993-1996
- New England Patriots – 1996-1997
- New York Jets – 1998
- Pro Bowl – 1993
- All-Pro – 1990
- Philadelphia Eagles
  - 75$^{th}$ Anniversary Team

**Pepper Johnson grew up in Michigan, played high school football in Michigan, but became one of the all-time great linebackers at The Ohio State University. Here are some of Pepper's thoughts on "The Rivalry:"**

"I'm in all sports, period. Because we do not do anything with this even after Michigan. You got to be, the teammates and all that stuff, but you see them. I have a Michigan attorney. I have a Michigan financial adviser and we play golf, and they lose and they put on Ohio State gear. Love it. I love it.

"Oh my goodness, yes. They call me Benedict Arnold. I was 17 years old and they called me Benedict Arnold. Jim

Spadafore, I still remember his name. He was a writer for the *Detroit Free Press*, and he called me Benedict Arnold. Because I was the top defensive player leaving the state of Michigan.

"But it's just great, Michigan has like 10 or 15 of Ohio players every year.

"We at Ohio State have one or two and it's like, that we're some bad guys. Well, yes. But I had to leave. I had to leave Michigan. It was growing up in the streets of Detroit and Ann Arbor was too close and they were, and Michigan was changing guys for that year and doing all that stuff like that. You know, I had a couple of guys before me that were All Americans and they changed their positions. Bill McCartney told me he was recruiting me. He was the Defensive Coordinator there. He left during the recruitment and became the head coach of Colorado.

"He called me back when he was still the defensive coordinator at Michigan, he said, 'No. They weren't planning on playing me at tight end and not thinking about.' Soon as he got the head coach job at Colorado, he called me and said, 'Yeah, Michigan wants you to be a tight end.' [laughs] I love it."

## Pepper Johnson

- Ohio State Football – 1982-1985
- Ohio State Starting Inside Linebacker – 1983-1985
- Ohio State – Lead team in tackles – 1984, 1985
- Ohio State Team Captain – 1984, 1985

- Ohio State Most Valuable Player = 1984, 1985
- All American Inside Linebacker 1985
- Ohio State Varsity O Hall of Fame in 2001
- New York Giants (1986-1992)
- Cleveland Browns (1993-1995)
- Detroit Lions (1996)
- New York Jets (1997-1998)

One of the more interesting times within the Ohio State vs Michigan Rivalry was during 1987, when OSU Head Coach, Earle Bruce, was fired by then Ohio State President Edward Jennings, going over OSU Athletic Director, Rick Bay's head and firing Earle the week before the game. Rick Bay, with all character and integrity, resigned in protest and All American Chris Spielman cites carrying Earle Bruce off the field in Michigan Stadium after beating the Wolverines, as his greatest memory as a Buckeye.

**Rick Bay gives his sentiments on the Ohio State/Michigan Rivalry and specifically on his experiences when Head coach Earle Bruce was fired prior to the 1987 game in Ann Arbor:**

"Oh, gosh. It was certainly a moment. I guess, ironically, the worst moment and the best moment. That is, Earle and I leaving, but then beating Michigan. In a way, the best and the worst happened in the same week, or even in the same day, because it was our last game. That was the worst thing, but the best thing was under those circumstances, to go to Ann Arbor and beat Michigan. With the fired coaching staff and program that was suddenly in disarray because of what had happened, to rally and put all that aside and go out and beat the favorite Michigan team in Ann Arbor was pretty darn special. That was certainly one of the highlights. Another great highlight for me was simply being named Athletic Director at Ohio State. It was an unexpected scenario, to say the least, given my Michigan background. It was a very proud moment for me, even the way things ended. It was the best job I ever had. I've had a bunch of them. I've remained to have a great fondness for Ohio State.

"I don't know if you know they're doing a documentary on Earle.

"I went down to Columbus to be with Earle and reminisce in front of the cameras and went to a game and we were out in the field of when Earle dotted the I in Script Ohio. That was another special moment to see that. After the way Earle was treated in the final season despite his great success to have it come full circle and to him having that singular honor of dotting the i. That was a great moment as well.

"I never had an angry word with Ed Jennings who ultimately made the decision. It was the way it was handled that was certainly not good. It wasn't justified, but it was civilized to some degree.

"I know it was just a terrific experience for me. I still take great pride in the fact that I'm one of the few guys around that has both Michigan and Ohio State background and has been a part of championship teams in both places if you can count administrators as part of the championship team. When I coached the championship team at Michigan, I was a champion myself when I wrestled. I'm proud of that combination for sure. When I was down with Urban Meyer, I guess early last fall, the coach was good enough to take me through the Woody Hayes Athletic Facility and have me talk to his coaches about how Earle was fired that day. Because a lot of those coaches don't have that history. They were brought in from other places or else they were too young to remember what happened in 1987. That was special. Walked around with Urban and be a part of a special day with the coach. I'm glad you called me. It's a great project you're working on. Certainly, the Ohio State feeling, as we said, it goes on forever. Even with a Michigan guy like me, it goes on forever. I'll never forget my time at Ohio State. It was wonderful." **Buckeyes for Life!**

# Rick Bay

- Michigan Football and Wrestling – 1961-1966
- Michigan's head wrestling coach – 1970-1974
- University of Oregon Athletics Director – 1981-84
- Ohio State University Athletics Director – 1984-87
- University of Minnesota Athletics Director – 1988-91
- San Diego State University Athletics Director – 1995-2003
- Executive Vice President and Chief Operating Officer – New York Yankees – 1988
- President and Chief Executive Officer – Cleveland Indians – 1991, 1992

*One person who has "inside the ropes" views on "The Game" is none other than Glen Shemy Schembechler. As the son of legendary Michigan coach, Bo Schembechler, Shemy honors us with his views and experiences of the greatest rivalry in North American sports and the "Ten Year War:"*

"You have to take a historical perspective, because I was born in September of the first year of the 'Ten Year War' in 1969. So, my understanding of the series didn't come about until later in my life, when I was given the opportunity to go back and study the significance of the "Ten Year War".' So, for years, you're a young kid and you're an idiot and you don't know anything. I remember from the age of five up until I was ten years old, we had a casket with Woody in it. We had a casket with a doll of Woody laying in a casket with pins riddled through the dolls body. It was almost like we carried around Ohio State in effigy with the fan base. It was always interesting to me how my dad didn't want to be a part of that. Like, 'You guys do what you want to do. We're getting ready to play Ohio State and if we don't beat Ohio State, the world is coming to an end, but we're not going to do all this effigy crap like you guys like to do.'"

Shemy says, "When we won the 69 game and all these guys were like, 'We can burn Woody in effigy whenever we want to,' but my old man would never be a part of that. They would bring the casket over to the house and we would have it at our tailgate before the games. So, here's little Shemy, not understanding the whole relationship between my dad and Woody, and you don't appreciate it until you can look at the big picture as to what it is all about. The whole thing didn't come into perspective for me until after Woody was done coaching.

"They taped the 'Ten Year War' and actually did the last episode at Doyt Perry's house on Bowling Green and my dad said to Woody, 'You're not in coaching anymore, you're mainly making public speeches, and you haven't been up to the house, you haven't been up to Ann Arbor,' and so Woody accepts the offer and it's a beautiful spring afternoon, I want to say 1981. So, Woody was going through type two diabetes therapy at that time and he had a driver, and they drive up to our place at 870 Arlington in Ann Arbor and they don't even pull into the driveway. They pull the car right in front of the front yard, and Woody gets out of the back seat, and my Dad is all excited, so he meets him halfway between the street and our front porch and he reaches his hand out to shake Woody's hand and he's so excited to see the 'Old Man' and Woody grabs his hand and looks him right in the eye and says, 'Bo, I didn't come here to see you.' And he walks right past my old man. My mom, Millie, is waiting on the front porch, and I'm standing right next to her and he says, 'Mrs. Shembechler, thanks so much for having me here,' and my mom lights up with the most beautiful smile, cause Woody was always so good with the moms and that was why he was such an outstanding recruiter and here's little Shemy and I'm thinking how much do I love Woody Hayes, because I had never met him in person, and to see him, how he was with my dad and my mom, it's a memory I will carry with me for the rest of my life. It instilled great respect, not only for this great relationship that my dad had with Woody, and how much he loved Woody, but how much that built the rivalry."

## Shemy Schembechler

- Son of HOF Coach Bo Schembechler
- President and Founder of GES Advisory Company
- 16 Year NFL Scout with the Chiefs, Bears, Redskins and Seahawks
- University of Michigan Football Recruiting Coordinator 1993-1995

BUCKEYES FOR LIFE

# "The Rivalry"
### (Images of the Passion and Intensity)

*Not only is the intensity of the Ohio State VS Michigan rivalry reflected on this page, but take a look at the respect and compassion in the upper right photo, where Michigan player, Devin Gardner prays for and comforts Ohio State quarterback J.T. Barrett after his leg was broken.*

TOM LEVENICK

# "The Rivalry"
## (Levity from Buckeye and Wolverine Fans)

The Ohio State VS Michigan game of 1973 was one of the greatest games in college football history. This year marks the 45th anniversary of that great, yet controversial contest, where the Buckeyes and Wolverines tied 10 to 10. Ohio State was then chosen to go to the Rose Bowl in an unprecedented vote by Big Ten Athletic directors.

Recently, I had the opportunity to visit with many Ohio State greats as well as a few from TSUN regarding that game and their experiences.

Regarding the 1973 Ohio State team, let us remember that team had lost only twice in four years, both to Michigan State. They had already played in three consecutive Rose Bowls.

The 1973 Ohio State vs. Michigan football game, played November 24th, was one of the most controversial games in NCAA history. In this game, both teams were undefeated, with Ohio State ranked 1st, and Michigan ranked 4th. The Buckeyes had outscored their opponents by an average of 37 points per game. A conference championship, Rose Bowl appearance, and possible national championship were on the line in this monumental game, part of the hotly contested stretch of the rivalry known as "The Ten-Year War." A then-NCAA record crowd of 105,233 watched the game at Michigan Stadium in Ann Arbor.

As the teams took the field, the rivalry game got off to an even more heated beginning, when the Buckeyes, led by John Hicks, stormed the field and tore down the famous "M–Go Blue" Letterman's Club banner. The Wolverines ran under and jumped up to touch that banner ceremoniously as they ran onto the field before each game in Michigan Stadium. Needless to say, the 105,233 fans in attendance that day, roared their disapproval.

Many reported that heavy rain prior to the game was the reason the battle was mostly fought on the ground. Michigan had 90 yards passing and Ohio State attempted only seven passing plays in a defensive contest.

Buckeye Quarterback Cornelius Green actually had a broken hand, unbeknownst to the public, which was a big reason for so few passes. The Buckeyes won the first half, leading 10 to 0 at the break. Michigan stormed back in the second half and they ended up tying 10 to 10.

Michigan's coaches and players felt that although the game was a tie, that they were the better team and deserved to go to the Rose Bowl. Even Ohio State coach Woody Hayes admitted that his team wouldn't go to the Rose Bowl. There was lots of debate on who would play in the Rose Bowl. Michigan's strong second half, and Franklin's injury were factors in debating who would represent the conference in the "granddaddy of them all." Ohio State had gone to the Rose Bowl the year before. The Big Ten at the time had a longstanding policy stating that only the conference champion would go to a bowl, the Rose Bowl. The Big Ten also had a "no-repeat" rule until 1971, and had it still been in effect, Michigan would have gone to the Rose Bowl automatically, even if it had *lost* to Ohio State. With the latter rule abolished, the decision as to who would represent the conference would be left up to a telephone vote by the Big Ten's athletic directors. According to Michigan coach Bo Schembechler's 1989 autobiography, the Big Ten was nervous because the conference had lost the previous four Rose Bowls, and Franklin's injury may have been a deciding factor

On the day after the game, following a conference call, it was announced that Ohio State would play in the Rose Bowl instead of Michigan. Schembechler was furious at the call, referring to it as "an embarrassment to the Big Ten Conference" and claiming "petty jealousies" were involved. Schembechler went on to demand changes to the Big Ten's policies regarding post-season play. He was particularly bitter because his 1973 team did not lose a game and was not rewarded with a bowl assignment and remained angry at the vote until his death in 2006. Schembechler also claimed the Franklin injury was just an excuse, since Ohio State's strength was a running game and not a passing attack.

**I have had a great opportunity to talk with many people who were involved in that historic game and here are some of their comments:**

*"I remember pre-game in the tunnel and I don't think we even thought about it at the time, but even though John Hicks won't admit to it, he led us out, and I believe John was the first one to grab the Michigan banner and the rest of the team joined in. It really ticked them off.*

*"My most vivid memory of that game was the toughness, but also the fact that we jumped out to an early lead, 10 to 0 and then got conservative with very limited passing. Corny Greene hurt his hand against Minnesota the week before and we didn't want to take any chances. So, we ran the ball the entire game and that was very predictable and we ended with a 10 to 10 tie. It was the only blemish on our season, which kept us from the National Championship.*

*"That might have been the greatest team we ever had at Ohio State. If you look at the numbers that we put out, they were ridiculous. And then we have to settle for a 10 to 10 tie. We didn't think we were going to be able to go to the Rose Bowl, and then when the Athletic Directors voted for Ohio State to go, we were elated. It gave us a chance to go out and avenge the loss we had to USC in the Rose Bowl the year before."*

**Archie Griffin**
Ohio State – Two-Time Heisman Trophy winner
– Starting Tailback

*"The 1973 Ohio State/Michigan game was the most intense game of our classic rivalry, at least what I remember of it. In the*

*middle of the third quarter, I had my 'bell rung' and I had staggered into the Michigan huddle. Randy Gradishar led me back to our huddle and I don't remember much after that.*

*"I do remember flying back from the game and Woody was so livid, he was banging his head on the side of the plane. It was a tough one to tie and we were one point away from winning the National Championship. Especially after the way we beat Southern Cal in the Rose Bowl."*

**Pete Cusick**
Ohio State - Starting Defensive Tackle, All-American, All- Big Ten 1973

*"It was one of the greatest playing experiences of my life. It was one we should have won, but we then went out and redeemed ourselves against USC in the Rose Bowl."*

**Randy Gradishar**
Ohio State – Starting Middle Linebacker, All-American 1973

*"It was the greatest game in Ohio State/Michigan history. I remember how excited we were to play that game as we ran out of the tunnel and the next thing I knew, the Michigan banner was coming down on top of me. I had nothing to do with pulling it down."*

**John Hicks**
Ohio State – Starting Offensive Tackle, Outland Trophy 1973, Lombardi Trophy 1973, 1st Person on the M-Club Banner

*"At Michigan, both teams come out of the same tunnel. I remember before the game, Woody said, "Put on your helmets*

*and buckle up those chinstraps, cause we're going to take on those SOBs right here in the tunnel."*

*We were so fired up, that when the ABC Sports official pointed to the team and said two minutes until you take the field, we just bolted out of the tunnel right then and there. Hicks absolutely grabbed that banner and we all piled on."*

*"The biggest thing I remember from the 73 Michigan game was that I got crushed on the opening kickoff. I had led the team in tackles on kickoffs that season and I was running down the field after the kick, in my lane and I had the return man dead to rights. That's when a guy clipped me. I dislocated my ankle and broke my tibia. Doctor Bob is taking care of me on the sidelines when Woody comes up and says, 'How is he?' Dr. Bob just shook his head NO. Woody then said 'He can't punt then?' Dr. Bob said NO again, when Woody said, 'How about kickoffs?' I was just crying laughing, even though I was hurt bad.*

*"After the game, we found out that play was in Michigan's plan to try to get me out of the game and damage our kicking game."*

**Tom Skladany**
Ohio State – Starting Kicker (Kickoffs) and Punter


*"We're down in the tunnel and all the fans are cheering and we see the M-Club guys with the banner out on the field and Woody says, "Go get that goddamn thing!" We run out and Hicks jumps up on the thing and all our guys pile on. They didn't really show it on TV, but it turned into a real slugfest."*

**Larry Romanoff**
Ohio State – 1973 Team Manager, Current Ohio State Associate Athletic Director

*"After 40 years, while trying to go back and find the guys who held the M-Club banner that game, I have not been able to find them. At Michigan, we only want to forget that day."*

**Laura Melvin**
Michigan – Former President of the M-Club

"We never heard about the banner being torn down until after the game, but Hicks still denied it to his last day. It was great to have the opportunity to play in the greatest rivalry in college football and the 1973 game was a 'bloodbath.' We were stunned when the Big Ten Athletic Directors voted for Ohio State to go. Using my broken collarbone as an excuse was a cop out. We knew we were the better team and the Ohio State players knew it too. Once the Athletic director vote came out, it was the first time I ever saw Bo Schembechler at a loss for words. He had to tell us we were not going to the Rose Bowl and he couldn't tell us why. He was livid and he was stunned.

"Ohio State and Michigan players are cut from the same cloth, intense, disciplined and ultra-competitive. I still stay in touch with some of the Ohio State players like Steve Luke and Archie Griffin. It's pretty cool to have the only two-time Heisman trophy winner as a good friend."

## Dennis Franklin

- Michigan - 1973 starting quarterback

After the athletic director vote and I believe as a result of many of Schembechler's protests, the Big Ten made changes to their bowl selection processes. Among the changes that were made in were the abolishment of the archaic "Rose Bowl or No Bowl" rule. This would allow conference teams other than the champion to accept invitations to other bowls. Michigan would be the first team to receive such an invite, to the Orange Bowl following the 1975 season.

**The Buckeyes proved the Big Ten athletics director's vote was correct when they went on to destroy USC, 42 to 21, in the Rose Bowl.**

The 10 to 10 tie denied Ohio State the national championship. Alabama vaulted the Buckeyes into the top spot in both polls, and the Crimson Tide finished the regular season 11-0 to earn the number one ranking in the UPI coach's poll, which did not conduct a post-bowl poll at that time. Notre Dame ended up as AP national champions by defeating Alabama, 24-23, in the Sugar Bowl, leaving the Buckeyes second in both wire-service surveys.

To this day, the aftermath of the 1973 Michigan-Ohio State contest remains one of the biggest controversies in college football history.

**Kirk Herbstreit shares his Michigan stories:**

"We tied them in '92 and John Cooper said in his postgame press conference, 'Herbie, that one was for you!' Coach Cooper and I have always had a good friendship. Once I got through, he and I are real tight right now. I remember walking off the field in my senior year and we tied them and I was bawling like a baby, just because I never got a chance to beat them. We had outplayed them that day and just for whatever reason, couldn't find a way to close the door. It was just all that stuff about the childhood and wearing a uniform and now here I am walking off the field against that team for the last time. It was all coming back emotionally for me. I think Cooper recognized that and he probably felt as bad as anybody that I was never able to knock them off.

"I felt bad for Cooper and he had great teams. It was like a metal hump, I think, for a lot of his teams. He just couldn't quite knock off Michigan even though there were many times they outplayed them on any given year.

**John Arbeznik played offensive guard for the Wolverines in the late 70s as I played offensive tackle for the Buckeyes in the late 70s and early 80s.**

Fast forward to 1994 and Arbeznik and I "happen upon" one another at a Wal-Mart convention in Omaha, Nebraska. John is there representing Earth Grains, while I am representing the Winterbrook Beverage Group. As strangers, we are sitting next to one another in the hallway, waiting for the next presentation to begin, when I look over and see Arbeznik's Big Ten Championship ring, just as John looks over and sees my

Big Ten Championship ring. We get acquainted and begin to share Ohio State and Michigan stories, Woody and Bo stories when we realize all of our experiences and daily routines were exactly the same. I shared the story that every week, we would practice in full pads Monday, Tuesday, and Wednesday for MICHIGAN, beating the hell out of one another, and then, Thursday and Friday we would have easier practices in sweat suits—no pads and put in Purdue's plays and the go out Saturday and beat them 46 – 6. We did that every week, no matter who we were playing.

Arbeznik just laughed and shook his head and then said, "We did the EXACT SAME THING! No wonder all those games in the 70s were always so close! We could have changed uniforms, Bo told me that years later. We could've literally switched uniforms and gone on the other side. It's the same program, it's the same pride, it was the same discipline. We had the same 14 traps, the reverse. Everything was identical, same formations.

No doubt, I mean we definitely knew that. Then also, the coaching strategies were, you get control of the clock, get a score, get a lead. You just don't turn it over.

Bo was amazing. When you graduated, he was certainly a pleasure, but when you played for him, he was really tough.

By the way, and you think the players are afraid of him. The coaches were terrified of him. That was him, though. Bo and Woody's secret was that they coach coaches and that's something that doesn't happen much today. You don't see a lot of that. When you see coaches getting friendly, they're not as good."

"There's an example of why a great coach today is still in control of his staff. A lot of these guys become buddies. That was the problem with Rodriguez while he was at Michigan, he was everybody's friend. You've got to be a prick. I know that sounds crazy, but just do the math on it. Look where the head coach is really in charge. You think he's taking direction from anybody? No, he's giving it. Then look at the weak coaches. It's unbelievable and that's the secret of Bo and Woody right there. Everybody's going to fear them. Everybody. Including me, except for the secretaries and stuff. The women that worked for him were always treated well. It's crazy.

"Just the reality of the Ohio State/Michigan game was that it was a one game season. You knew at the end of the season, that game was for the Rose Bowl certainly. Every year but one it was for the Rose Bowl for us and in that period. One of those years, we were third place and what happened was that if Purdue lost and we beat Ohio State, then we would have gone so I guess technically it was always for the Rose Bowl.

"The other thing was—I'm not sure that the league was as dominant back then. They talked about 'The Big Two and the Little Eight,' so, the fact that we met all those years together I think had to do with the fact that almost all the Midwestern talent was that at Ohio State in Michigan, which made it a different dynamic than today, because of that you had super teams playing each other. There's all your best players from Midwest or from Ohio were on either of our teams—and that's the other thing, we had a lot of Ohio kids in Michigan back then and you don't see that today anymore.

"I remember when Dan Dierdorf, former Michigan player and NFL Hall of Famer, said one time on national TV, he says, 'You know, back when I was recruited,' and he was from Canton, Ohio. He says, 'Back when I was recruited, if your first choice was Michigan, your second choice was Ohio State and if your first choice is Ohio State, your second choice was Michigan.' Back then we had 120 scholarships. Now they got 85 and so if you look at it there's 35 guys from Michigan and 35 from Ohio State that now go elsewhere. Now you see the Michigan States and the Pittsburghs and the Penn States and everybody that's better than they used to be because the talent is spread out.

"There's more parity. I still think Ohio State and Michigan are the cream of the crop in the Big Ten, but Wisconsin's snuck in there every now and then and I'm a little surprised at Nebraska, they've been good but they just haven't been how Nebraska used to be.

"I just remember how clean played it was," Arbeznik said. "There wasn't cheap shot. I'll tell you, my senior year I got cheap shotted in the Navy game. Navy was the worst, and there was a lot of under the piles stuff. It was unbelievable. The four years I played in the Ohio State/Michigan Game, it was always the cleanest played game. I don't know if it was because we were all scared to death of Bo and Woody. [chuckles] I suspect that's the case.

"The referees were always impressed with the sportsmanship. We wanted to beat the hell out of each other and it was the toughest game, but there was nothing ever that was surprising. We had the same premise, we're just going to run you over and our idea was the same thing, you, we're going to run over us. It was just a physically hard game. There is nothing—nothing was new. There was no twist to that. If you beat your man, I beat mine. Everybody beats their man, you win the game. I really don't care in the rollover which was the key. It was really boring football. The three yards and a cloud of dust is probably the perfect description of it, but that's their intention of it.

"Back then, we had a lot of great Ohio players playing at Michigan. Great players starting with Charles Woodson, Rob Lytle or whether it was Tom Darden or Desmond Howard. We had so many great players from Ohio that came up when I was playing. Schmerge from Cincinnati, became all pro at Miami from Woodville. You could just make an NFL all-star team. An all time all-star team out of just the Ohio State or Ohio kids who went to Michigan. I don't think you can do that for Ohio from Michigan. I don't think Michigan had enough to send enough guys down there, but it just showcased the fact that Ohio was a center of high school football, no doubt about it. Nobody's going to argue that anyway in the Midwest.

"They say Texas, but Texas is six times the size of Ohio. Let's say California, the same thing, and they'll say Florida and that's mostly skill position. It's Ohio high school football by far.

"You're going to see this, now that Harbaugh is back, this rivalry is about to really pick up and this is going to get majorly intense. The Bo, Woody thing was easy. That's when I played, so it's hard for me to go unrehearsed, but this era, right now, is going to get nuts. My Ohio State friends are all saying the same thing. They always wanted to have Michigan undefeated and highly ranked. They wanted us to be number two or three because they wanted to beat us, so it helps them in the national polls too. When you beat a good Michigan team you guys are trying to get in the playoffs and get to the number one spot too. It didn't do you any good when we were five and six with Rich Rodriguez. Beating an average Michigan team while there were other big games going on around the country that day, you guys wouldn't get in.

"I think that's changed. I think we're getting national recruiting back. I think recruiting in the state of Ohio's about to heat up. This is going to get down and nasty. I think the next 10 years. I think we're in a fair fight now. I don't think we were the last 10 years if that makes sense to you. Before, when we had Rodriguez in there, I was embarrassed.

"When Justin Boren transferred from Michigan to Ohio State, that was tough on the rivalry for us. Mike Boren was an incredible Wolverine. That whole family was geared and ready to go to Michigan and something happened. Michigan lost its way in that 10-year period in the Ohio State Michigan War. Guys like the Borens, we offended them and they're sending all their kids to Buckeye Land now.

"The soul of what we were losing in the rivalry was when those things started happening. We were losing our identity with our alumni and our past players because we were bringing in coaches that had no ties back to Michigan.

"People like Mike Boren's family were, and his son, who like that one coach, the kid had just transferred to Ohio State a couple years ago. That was a glaring problem that the Ohio State-Michigan transfer situation went to Ohio State because, Ohio State was a better place to go. It was more stable. You're going to win championships. That's the thing we're trying to get back.

"The whole thing is about getting the series back. I can't sit there for 10 years and lose to Ohio State like they're doing now. It's the same way my friends, when I was in the nineties, I'd go to Columbus. When we were beating the Ohio State in that run. One thing I didn't do, I never trash talked them. Never once. Matter of fact, I used to love Coach Hayes. I respected him like you don't even know. I would just bring up the good things of Woody's when they were trashing Woody in Columbus.

"Years later it helped me because I played and I actually had a good reputation in Columbus because of my respect for Ohio State. We now feel we're back. We feel we finally can be competitive. We feel we can be #1 and #2 again. Not next year, maybe two years. It's going to get intense. I think it's great for the both of us."

## John Arbeznik

- Michigan Football 1976-1979
- First-team All-Big Ten Conference offensive guard – 1978-1979.

**While "The Rivalry" exists mainly in the sport of football, Buckeye Swimming Great, Teresa Fightmaster experienced "The Rivalry" in Women's Swimming as well.**

"We respect Michigan, but we also love to hate each other," Fightmaster said. "That's the rivalry and that's what makes it fun, though, too.

"Our swimming coach, Jim Montrella, every away meet we went to, he would make us walk around the campus before the swimming competition because he wanted us not to just see the pool, but he wanted us to see the campus. I remember one meet we were up in Ann Arbor. It was January, it was cold, we're walking around their park as a team and all of a sudden, people started throwing snowballs at us. We were so upset and he would not let us throw them back at them. I'm just like, 'Are you kidding me?' That was one of the memories we had. We won the meet and had the last laugh!"

## Teresa Fightmaster

- The Ohio State University 1982-1986
- Ohio State University – 5-time NCAA All-American
- Ohio State University – 3-time Individual Big Ten Champion
- Ohio State University – 4 year All- Big Ten selection
- Ohio State University – Big Ten Record Holder 50 Yard Breaststroke
- Ohio State University – Co-Captain
- Ohio State University – National Team member at the World Student Games in 1983

# 8

# "THE BEST DAMN BAND IN THE LAND"

## (Paired with the TEAM)

The Ohio State Football Team and The Ohio State University Marching Band have a terrific relationship based on mutual excellence. Coach Woody Hayes coined the term, "The Best Damn band in the Land" back in 1968 and they have answered to that nickname ever since.

It was during John Cooper's tenure as Buckeye Head Coach that the "Tunnel of Pride" was created. Created by former OSU quarterback Rex Kern and former Director of Athletics Andy Geiger, the Tunnel of Pride started in 1995, when Notre Dame visited Ohio Stadium for the first meeting between the two teams in nearly 50 years. Former Buckeye football players form a tunnel, along with the Ohio State University Marching Band for the team to run through as it runs onto the field. This tradition has now continued every other year when Michigan visits Ohio Stadium.

Each year, as a former player, during the Tunnel of Pride, I get a tear in my eye and the hair raises on the back of my neck as I get to relive the experience with teammates and the band in front of 107,000 terrific fans.

When Jim Tressel took over as head coach of the Buckeyes, things began to change even more.

I will never forget, during the postgame award ceremony, when the Buckeyes won the National Championship in 2002 and Tressel said, "We've always had the Best Damn Band in the Land. Now, we have the Best Damn Team in the Land!"

Tressel was instrumental in expanding the relationship between the band and the football team when he began his career as head coach of the Buckeyes in 2001. During his initial days, he met with the band director at that time, Dr. Jon Woods and asked to start a new tradition, where the team sings the Alma Mater, with the band at the end of each game.

Back in the 1970s and 80s, another tradition was the band came out to football practice during Michigan week each year and played all the fight songs from the sidelines during practice. That tradition changed during John Cooper's tenure as head coach as the band continues to play during a Michigan Week practice, but they now perform the "Incomparable Script Ohio" and the football team marches with the band!

I spoke recently with the new Band Director of the Ohio State University Marching Band, Dr. Christopher Hoch. Hoch was quick to praise Jim Tressel and also Buckeye Head Coach Urban Meyer.

"Coach Tressel fully understood the wonderful relationship between the band, the fans, the cheerleaders, the athletic department, and the football players themselves," Hoch said. "Now, Coach Meyer has kept those traditions going and truly values the role that the band plays... He will occasionally come to our band meetings and give a pep talk to the members. It is a wonderful relationship."

## Dr. Christopher Hoch

- Director of the Ohio State University Marching Band – 2016-Present
- Ohio State Bachelor's Degree – Music Education and mathematics – 2000
- Ohio State Master's Degree – Instrumental Conducting and Music Education – 2002
- Ohio State Ph.D. – Music Education – 2012

It is incredible to watch Coach Meyer and his wife, Shelley, as they sing Carmen Ohio with the team after each game. The joy and happiness they exhibit for each other, the band, the team and the tradition is inspiring.

Urban Meyer, just like Tressel wants to help his players understand there is more to their college experience than just football. He wants to educate his players on the traditions of the school and most importantly make his players proud of the University they represent.

Urban and Shelley singing Carmen Ohio    Urban pre-game speech to the Band

While I was a student athlete at The Ohio State University, I was lucky to have created a friendship with my R.A. at

Steeb Hall, Craig Kossuth. Craig had been a two-year member of TBDBITL as a T-Row Trumpet player and he and I used to tease each other quite frequently regarding which team practiced longer and harder, the Marching Band or the Football team.

Craig was so proud to have been a member of the band and shared with me many of the long hours and tasks that the band members endured in order to deliver an impeccable show each Saturday afternoon.

Similar to the football team, the band practiced two plus hours a day. They watched film of previous game performance and tryouts and they had "Challenge Day" every Monday. "Challenge Day ensures we have the best band on the field every Saturday delivering the best performance," Kossuth said. "There are 12 members and two alternates to each row in the band and each Monday those alternates can challenge any member of their row in a competition to see who knows and plays that week's music better. It kept us on our toes."

The NCAA now limits the football team to 20 hours of practice a week, but when I played football in the late 70s and early 80s, we spent around 50 hours a week divided between practice, meetings, film work, and study table.

"Seriously and all teasing aside, I don't know how you guys did it," Kossuth said. I used to see how beat up you'd get and wonder how you accomplished your studies after such a long physical day."

Just like many of the former football players with whom we have spoken, Craig has incredible memories of his TBDBITL days. "I will never forget my first ramp entrance into Ohio Stadium," Craig said.

"Coming out of that tunnel in front of 90,000 fans, being a member of the Best Damned Band in the land and then hearing "The Pride of the Buckeyes," the Ohio State University Marching Band, caused a chill to run down my spine." Craig also played for the band in the 1976 Orange Bowl and the

1977 Sugar Bowl. "They were the greatest experiences in my life, he said.

As a former player, I can tell you that each and every one of us is proud of the university we represented, The Ohio State University. Just as important, we are proud of the band, the traditions and environment they create, and the excellence

with which they perform. It mirrors the goals of the football team and it is a true sense of pride for all alumni, just as we, the Buckeye Football Team always strive to be.

While the relationship between the Best Damn Band in the Land and the Ohio State Buckeyes has changed over the years, the pageantry, the tradition, and the pride has not. Some things will never change. **Buckeyes for Life!**

## *Jack Nicklaus "Dots the I" of Script Ohio!!!*

## JACK NICKLAUS

- Ohio State Golf 1959 – 1961
- NCAA Championship – Ohio State won: 1961
- U.S. Amateur – Won: 1959, 1961
- Masters Tournament – Won: 1963, 1965, 1966, 1972, 1975, 1986
- U.S. Open – Won: 1962, 1967, 1972, 1980
- The Open Championship
  - Won: 1966, 1970, 1978
- PGA Championship
  - Won: 1963, 1971, 1973, 1975, 1980

***Cardiff Hall Share some great memories of TBDBITL:***

"Yes, absolutely. I was thinking about this going in and those college stories that happened. But my freshman year, Tom, there was the Thursday before the Michigan game - that Michigan game was in Ann Arbor - Thursday night was something that they did called Phantom Pep Night. I don't know. Did you do those back then when you were playing.

"This is going to be a little different. This is at midnight. It was close to midnight, maybe eleven o'clock, we met. I would say not all the band members did, but a large majority of them met at the VC. That's where we kick this off. We're going to march around the campus, and we're going to fire everybody up. We meet at the VC, we play the fight song, *Hang on Sloopy,* all the school songs. The team then march—well, not the team, the group. And this group now is probably the band, let's say it's around 50 to 75 to 80 people. All the instruments are represented. We head up to North Campus and we play at—What's the first—Drackett? Whatever the first residential building is.

"It was Drackett. We start playing the fight song, *Hang on Sloopy.* Lights start going on. Students start looking at the windows. They start to cheer. We then go from there to the next group of buildings, and as we're going along now, people are coming out of their dorms, and they're following us. So, we're waking students up, they're putting on their stuff. We're following people now. We got a big group of people. And we go up to—is it Larkin? We go up to the one—We're marching up with that Woody Hayes—so we're going up Woody Hayes, we're stopping, we're playing in front of—what is that? By that church, the group of dorms that are by that church.

"Now, we have a bigger following now. This has grown into a very large crowd. Again, firing the students up. The students are actually getting toilet paper and toilet-papering the trees. Then we go from North Campus to down to South

Campus and then we're on that side street that's parallel to High Street, and we're marching, and we're playing. Now we've got a horde of students behind us. North Campus doing the support—now we're at the South Campus. We played the first South Campus dorm, same thing happens.

"Lights are going on, students are cheering, they come down [laughs]. It is completely chaos. It's crazy. Students are fired up because Michigan game is coming up.

"Then we go to Mirror Lake, and then the band is by the lake, students start jumping into the lake. It was pandemonium. It was unbelievable. The path that we went in was covered by toilet paper. Trees got toilet-papered. It was like Sherman's March back in the day. That one experience was amazing. That one pops into my head. I've never seen anything like it.

"Students would be sleeping, getting up, following the band, cheering on the band. We go North Campus to South Campus. It was incredible. It was called Phantom Pep Night.

"That happens. That was when I was in my freshman year. Then we go up to Michigan, it is the coldest—this Earle Bruce's last game. This is Earle Bruce's last game, 19—would be '87. 1987 Michigan in Ann Arbor. And yes, oh gosh, we got the great linebackers, Spielman, he was the linebacker, it was a good team. But anyway, we get there. It is the coldest day, Tom, I have ever been a part of, a game experience.

"So, you probably remember. We get out and our valves are freezing. We're getting ready, we're at the stadium packing our instruments. The valves, because it's so cold, our valves are freezing. Now, there should not be any alcohol in collegiate anything. A group of people have Jim Beam and some other stuff. Everybody starts to put a little bit of Jim Beam in the valve and it works. We can play our valves because they're not sticky.

"So, we're playing, we do *Script Ohio* in the pregame. Of course, we win. They carry Earle Bruce off. I don't know on whose shoulder, but I remember that. Amazing experience. Then we do our postgame show, then Michigan has their show. We do our show, they were standing—actually, this story, Tom, is at halftime. We do our halftime show. It's freaking cold. My hands are like purple, man. We get off, and to be respectful of Michigan's band, we just crouch down. We kneel down in our military position and we listen to them. They do their performance, though. At the end of their performance, they played their fight song. Now, Ohio State, the marching band does not use any music. We had to memorize our music, we had to practice our music.

"We had to basically know our music. I'll never forget this. I think I'm on the 25-yard line. I'm looking, and I've got trumpet players looking up, playing their stuff. These trumpet players—everybody in Michigan has music, they're playing their fight song, Tom. They're playing, and then have to flip the page, because they don't know their fight song, I'm like, 'Are you kidding me?' They play this fight song so many times, they can't memorize it? They were flipping the pages like they didn't know their own fight song.

"That will stick out into my mind as, 'You know what? We are the best damn band in the land.' If you don't know your fight song at any school, you shouldn't be there. That got to me, man. That was incredible.

"During Michigan week, we would go to Woody Hayes facility, and we would do *Script Ohio*, I remember. We would actually give our instruments to the football players. They would have their pads on. They would be marching at *Script Ohio*, and it was the funniest thing. I can't remember who took my instrument, but all the players, we would give—I think it was seniors and juniors, we would give our instruments to the players and let them do the *Script Ohio*. It was awesome. It was just incredible. I do remember those experiences with the team.

"I 'Dotted the I' November 21st, 1990. First off, Tom, you have to be senior to 'Dot the I.' At the beginning of the football season, the band director will come up to whoever had the most points. Points meaning whoever has marched the most on the field, not as an alternate, whoever has done these various things. I was never an alternate, Tom. I worked my butt off. I got challenged once, and I smoked the guy. I smoked him. No one ever challenged me again. No one did in four years. I was challenged in my freshman year for my position. I won. For the next four years, no one ever challenged me again. So, I had the most points as a senior."

## CARDIFF D. HALL

- Graduate of The Ohio State University – 1991
- BSBA Major in Logistics and Marketing.
- The Ohio State University Marching Band "I" Dotter 1990
- Author of Tide Turners and President Inspiration Insight

**One of Pepe Pearson's greatest experiences in his football career at Ohio State involved the Ohio State University Marching Band:**

"One of the off the field experiences that I enjoyed was one of the traditions where the band would come to our practice during 'Michigan Week' and we would position ourselves each with a different band member and music instrument and march with the band as they performed Script Ohio. That was pretty cool for me because it engaged a different part of what Ohio State is because Script Ohio has so much tradition and they've been doing it for years that it was very special to me to be a part of that. We marched around with them and did Script Ohio, each of us with a different band member, for instance, I was with the Drum Major. It was a great experience to be a part of that."

## PEPE PEARSON

- Ohio State Football 1993 – 1996
- Four-year Letter winner – Running Back
- Starter – 1997 Rose Bowl victory over Arizona State
- Marshall University – Running Backs Coach

TOM LEVENICK

# "TBDBITL meets the Team"
## (Images of Michigan Week – "Meet the Team Night")

**Bob Atha, former Buckeye Kicker, shares a great memory of the band for us:**

"One of my great memories would be pretty obvious, when I kicked five field goals against Indiana in 1981 to break the school record, but an even greater memory was from the Rose Bowl in 1980," Atha said. "You'll remember that Frank Sinatra was the Grand Marshall of the Rose Parade and the Rose Bowl. So, we run out of the tunnel to start the game and the band is just coming off the field and there is a lot of commotion on the sideline and as I am running onto the field amongst the band, I bump into 'Old Blue Eyes' himself. Sinatra sticks out his hand and we shake hands and he says, 'Play a good game today, son.' That was a pretty cool experience for a 19-year-old kid."

## BOB ATHA

- Ohio State Football 1978 – 1981
- Ohio State Backup Quarterback – 1978-1980
- Ohio State Starting Kicker – 81
- October 24, 1981 Ohio State vs Indianan Ohio Stadium
    - Atha made five field goals to set an Ohio State school record
- Miami Dolphins
- Arizona Cardinals

I told Atha that I had two stories like that. One was our freshman year when we ran out to the field at the end of halftime for our Homecoming game against Iowa. Drum Major Dwight Hudson was dotting the "I" with Bob Hope. Bob Hope walked off the field, and Woody grabbed him and pulled him in to the huddle. The first thing that Bob Hope did was reach out and shake my hand and said, "Good luck today, son." I shook Bob Hope's hand. Then, the next year we went to the Rose Bowl. The team went to Lawry's Prime Rib in Beverly Hills, and they have this prime rib-eating contest where they measure all the prime rib the whole team eats and the individuals eat. It was us against USC. All the proceeds go to the homeless and a homeless charity. Literally, I ended up winning the damn thing. I ate 10 and a half pounds of prime rib. The next evening as a team, we end up going to the Hollywood Palladium for the Big Ten Champion's Dinner and Bob Hope is the master of ceremonies. Billy Crystal is there. Loni Anderson is there and all these other stars. Bob Hope walks out on stage to begin the ceremony, and he goes, "Taaahhhhmmmmm Levenick!!!!!!!" Everybody looks at me as Hope says, "Man, if you can hold that burp till kick off, you guys will surely win." I'm like, "Oh, my God." I look over my shoulder, and my mother and father are hanging their heads. They are so disappointed in me.

**That same Drum Major, Dwight Hudson, who I believe was the best Drum Major ever at Ohio State shares some of his memories of "The Best Damn Band in the Land:"**

"Well, I tell you, one thing that stands out to the forefront right now is the Oklahoma game in 1977 when we played Oklahoma at Ohio State. You know how the band comes out first and forms a block, and then the drum major is the last one that comes out. They spread out. When I started to strut down the ramp to run out on the field, the crowd was so loud! I felt as if they were pushing me back in the tunnel. It was that loud. I was forcing myself through the sound of the crowd to get through the band to get to the front of the band. I just never will forget that. That was the loudest I've ever heard that stadium and the cheers for the band. When they saw me coming out of the tunnel, they just went berserk.

"Another one, of course, is going to the Rose Bowl, which you were at. I was asleep during the Rose parade
on the bus because the assistant drum major usually does the parade. Nowadays, I think they both do the parade. Back then when I was in school, it was a tradition that the assistant drum major does the parade and then the drum major does the game, so I did the game. But I was asleep, and when I woke up, I felt really refreshed. Lo and behold, I had the best game as far as no drops, not missing anything on my cues or anything. I had the best pre-game and halftime show that I ever had.

"Last, but not least, the 1979 Michigan game in Ann Arbor, and we win. That was your year where we were going to Rose Bowl. We win, and we're going to the Rose Bowl. The band, marched out of the stadium. At the time, the band director was Dr. Paul Droste. He had everybody turn around, face the stadium and play at the very loudest, *California, Here We Come.*"

TOM LEVENICK

## DWIGHT HUDSON

- Ohio State University Marching Band 1977 – 1979
- Ohio State Drum Major – 1977-1979

# 9

# "MOST MEMORABLE BUCKEYE EXPERIENCES"

## (Former players and coaches share their stories)

We all had so many great experiences as former players that it is difficult to single out just one. However, I have asked many former players to do just that, and I have come up with some great memories from some Great Buckeyes. We ate, slept, and drank football and worked hard on our education at The Ohio State University. We experienced blood, sweat, tears, and broken bones and also many victories and championships, which we reveled in and celebrated TOGETHER. Together, we became Buckeyes for Life!

"**I had so many great experiences at Ohio State,**" A.J. Hawk said.

"Winning the 2002 National Championship in the Fiesta Bowl against Miami was absolutely the greatest experience that I have ever had in football. Being able to play and contribute as a freshman on that team was an incredible feeling.

"I am also proud to have played in three Fiesta Bowls and the Alamo Bowl and we won them all," Hawk said. "I would be lying to you, though, if I didn't say that sacking my brother-in-law (Brady Quinn) twice in the 2005 Fiesta Bowl wasn't also a very special experience," Hawk said. It certainly gives me bragging rights whenever the entire family is together." (Hawk married Laura Quinn, sister of the former Notre Dame Quarterback. Hawk went on to play for the Green Bay Packers, Cincinnati Bengals, and Atlanta Falcons, while Quinn went on to play quarterback for the Seattle Seahawks).

"The greatest experiences in my life were at Ohio State, but I am most proud of the consistent level of excellence that Ohio State maintains. We're always at the top, we play by the rules and we do things the right way," A.J. said. Aaron James Hawk was obviously a great former Buckeye and a great NFL player for the Packers, Bengals, and the Atlanta Falcons. A.J. also holds a Bachelor of Arts degree in criminology and is interested in law enforcement following his NFL career. Something tells me that should A.J. Hawk pursue a career after football in law enforcement, we will all be better because of his efforts. *"Buckeyes for Life."*

## A.J. HAWK

- Ohio State Football 2001 – 2005
- Ohio State Starting Linebacker 2002 – 2005
- 2× Unanimous All-American – 2004, 2005

- Ohio State Buckeyes MVP – 1987
- Lombardi Award – 2005
- Jack Lambert Trophy – 2005
- Green Bay Packers – 2006–2014
- Cincinnati Bengals – 2015
- Atlanta Falcons – 2016
- Green Bay Packers
    - Super Bowl champion XLV

**Joey Bosa shares some recent Buckeye memories:**

"It was awesome to win the 2015 National Championship," Joey said. "I think that's really everybody's goal when they come to play at a high collegiate level, is to hold that trophy and win a National Championship and to come here and to reach all my goals. I mean getting that National Championship, but moving after three years and being the first-round pick in the NFL Draft, which was my goal. It's amazing as it happened so quickly and I'd have to say the best moment out there in three years was definitely holding up that trophy and celebrating with your teammates afterwards.

"I'll never forget giving Zeke (Ezikial Elliott) a big hug at the trophy presentation. It was—the moment we had been waiting for a really long time and just to be such a big part of it along with Zeke and us being close friends, the last two years. Being roommates and being such a big part of that win and that team that year. It was just an amazing feeling.

"I was at the 2017 spring game. I saw all the coaches. We relived the experience a little bit and I got to see Nicky play (younger brother Nick Bosa). I've been keeping in contact with Coach Meyer and Coach Johnson. I'm a Buckeye for Life."

## Joey Bosa

- Ohio State Football 2013 – 2015
- Ohio State Starting Defensive End – 2013 – 2015
- 2014 All-Big Ten
- 2014 – Big Ten Defensive Player of the Year
- 2014 – Big Ten Lineman of the Year
- 2014 – First Team All-American
- 2016 NFL Defensive Rookie of the Year – San Diego Chargers

**Keeping it "All in the Family" with Nick following his Uncle, Eric Kumerow, and older brother, Joey. Nick Bosa shares his greatest experience in his very successful, but young career as a Buckeye:**

"I would probably go with the win against Penn State last year. Just being down by 18 points and fighting back. We had leaders on the team, the older guys just never giving up and the last play of the game was a rushing package where the four defensive ends run go on the field and we closed it out. The whole stands rushed the field. It is just a great moment. We were all hugging and the old guys were crying and it kept that season alive and our goals alive. So, that was probably the best moment so far."

## NICK BOSA

- Ohio State Football 2016 – Present
- ESPN Freshman All-American (2016)
- First Team All-Big Ten (2017)
- Smith–Brown Big Ten Defensive Lineman of the Year (2017)
- Big Ten Champion (2017)

Nick Bosa played in all 13 games as a true freshman at Ohio State in 2016, recording 29 tackles, seven of which were for a loss, and five sacks. His sophomore year, he became the starting defensive end for the Buckeyes in seven games. Bosa was named a unanimous First Team All-Big Ten and the Smith-Brown Big Ten Defensive Lineman of the Year for his 32 total tackles (14.5 for a loss) and a team leading seven sacks.

**Katie Smith, certainly the greatest Women's Basketball player in Ohio State history and most likely, the greatest women's athlete on all fronts, performance, academics, paying forward, and life after Ohio State, shares her feelings about her greatest experience as a Buckeye:**

"My greatest experience was my freshman year, not necessarily one specific experience, but it was the whole year because it was very unexpected, the success that we had. We did have a highly ranked freshman class, but it was just the snowball effect of coming in as underdogs and not really knowing, and then having a game on national TV, winning the Big Ten and playing against Iowa, who was a powerhouse and making that run to the final four, and the championship game, and the fans.

"The camaraderie you have with your team, it's just that bond, and anytime you win as a team, you just have a connection that lives forever. It's just that whole—it's your first year in college at Ohio State, I'm an Ohio kid, and it was just the love that you got from the university and the fans. Then just the fun and experience of traveling, playing, competing with my teammates. It was incredible to me."

## Earle Bruce Shared some more great memories of his Buckeye days:

"I had a great experience at every one of the places I've coached, Bruce said. But let me put it into perspective. "When you graduate from Ohio State and you coach here and you played here, I actually got hurt playing – Everything is big here.

"Certainly, beating Iowa when they were undefeated and number one in the country and beating Michigan in 1979 was great, but for sure in 1987 after I was fired was incredible. To get fired on Monday and to win the biggest game in college football on Saturday, that just doesn't happen. That was about as exciting as anything could possibly be. The joy of that football game afterwards was a great memory.

(Earle was carried off the field by his players, in Michigan Stadium, after completing a 5-4 record vs. TSUN in nine years). "That's a tribute to the kids that played," Earle said.

"I've had a great career in coaching and a bunch of great football players. You don't win unless you have great football players and that's what it's all about." You win with people. **"Buckeyes for Life".**

**Chris Spielman shares his most memorable Buckeye experience:**

"Without question, it was the 1987 Michigan game when we beat Michigan in Ann Arbor and facing the tunnel, we carried Coach Earle Bruce off the field in his last game ever as the Ohio State head coach. It couldn't have been more fitting. The difference at Ohio State is the people," Spielman said. "We were one entity within a team - that is what that day was all about." ***Buckeyes for Life!***

**Keith Byars tries to share his best experience as a Buckeye:**

"I can't give you just one, but I'd still remember walking off the field after beating Michigan when we had won the Big Ten in 1984. I got three touchdowns, we beat them 21 to 6, and we're going to the Rose Bowl. Just to see the joy and adulation in our fans' eyes that could look down on the field, celebrating the Big Ten Championship because we haven't won the Big Ten Championship in a few years being at home. We won it in '81 at Michigan, but to win it at Ohio Stadium, in front of our home fans, it had been a while. They stormed the field. We're walking off. The last time they could see us in person in Ohio Stadium—that was special to me. Walking off the field. That's something that I will always remember — it has always stuck with me throughout the years."

"And of course, when you talk about Ohio State, Illinois, that was very special to me, but I'm sure it also was to a lot of my teammates when they sit back and think about it." (After trailing 24 – 0, Ohio State "roared back" behind 274 yards rushing and 5 touchdowns by Keith Byars, to win 45 – 28).

## Keith Byars

- *Ohio State Football 1983 – 1986*
- *Ohio State Starting Running Back 1984, 85, 86*
- *Ohio State Consensus All-American – 1984*
- *Ohio State – 2nd in voting for the Heisman – 1984*
- *Philadelphia Eagles – 1986-1992*
- *Miami Dolphins – 1993-1996*
- *New England Patriots – 1996-1997*
- *New York Jets – 1998*
- *Pro Bowl – 1993*
- *All-Pro – 1990*
- *Philadelphia Eagles*
  - *75th Anniversary Team*

**Roy Hall shares his most memorable experiences and like many "Young Bucks" for the 2000s, his great experiences are not too surprising:**

"I think number one is winning the National Title in 2002. I was a freshman that year, red-shirt freshman. You're a big-time recruit, you come in and you get a red-shirt, so you get a little bit discouraged because you want to come and play right away, but obviously, red-shirt doesn't necessarily mean you can't play, it just may mean that based on the way things shook out, it's just not necessary to have you on the field and waste the whole year eligibility for you. Just being able to be in position to learn how to win, to humble yourself and work hard and watch some of the seniors that year, the likes of Michael Doss, and Donnie Nickey, Kenny Peterson, Steve Grant, those guys came, and Tim Anderson. We had some great senior leaders that year, and we won a National Championship. You saw the sacrifice that Mike Doss made coming back for his senior year when he could've been a first-round draft pick in the NFL, just so he could win a National Title. That meant everything, because now, I get to talk about that even though I necessarily wasn't playing. I was on the sideline, I was dressed. You know how that goes when you red-shirt, and I added value to that team. Even on scout team, and pushing those guys ahead of you, and learning from those seniors and juniors. Michael Jenkins, Craig Krenzel on that squad. Chris Gamble was on that team, so we learned a lot. We learned how to win, which kind of set us up for the next four years, to play for the National Championship in 2006.

"Winning that first national title, beating Michigan 14-9 during my freshman year, is something that probably was the greatest team moment that I had at Ohio State because it was a National Title and because we shocked the world and showed what you can do when you've got the right pieces in place, and get the people that are willing to sacrifice for the betterment of the team."

**Pepper Johnson has some great memories of his experiences as a Buckeye:**

"I have one. When I heard both of them, but that one, when you say that, took my mind away from the first question, I don't know, there's so many equivalents. Because running out of the tunnel for that first ball game, running out of the tunnel was amazing to me. That was amazing to me. Meeting Woody Hayes, there's no way I can put words together on how that made me feel when I met him. Then I became a captain. Every week, he sat next to me. I told my son as much, it's that way before my son gets to Ohio State.

"I can't really put one of them ahead of the other. I wish I could. Beating the team up north. Beating the Ohio State Basketball team in a basketball scrimmage was one too. [laughter] I don't know. Having a son play football for Ohio State was a great experience too! That was amazing. I would say three weeks ago, we had our first father son autograph session in Columbus. That took it over the top. We both signed autographs at a sporting goods store. We sat down and I remember it was June 23rd because it was on my grandson's birthday that we got the okay from my son's coach that we could go and sign autographs. We went and signed autographs. That was the first time we did it together. I was excited. I was trying to have him keep an open mind when Ohio State was recruiting him and everything. Well, he got so excited and I knew it was a done deal as soon as they told me that they were going to recruit him.

***Archie Griffin has a similar experience that is his most memorable as a Buckeye:***

"Probably, the most memorable experience other than the North Carolina game my freshman year is my last game that I played in Ohio Stadium. We came off the field. We played Minnesota and I will never forget when Woody brought all the seniors off the field one at a time so that the fans could say goodbye to each one of us.

To me that was very, very special because I think what he was saying to the fans is that these seniors were a special group, were a special part of the team, and those seniors never lost a game in Ohio Stadium and I think that's what he was trying to portray to the fans that he pulled us all off one person at a time. When we were on offense, getting towards the end of the game, before the game ended and we had a pretty good lead, he would pull Cornelius Green off, and then he pulled Brian Baschnagel off the field, somebody came in for them, and then he pulled me off at the very end. You talk about a memorable moment. That was a very, very, very memorable moment for me because certainly it was the last game that we were going to play together at home, but even more importantly, I felt that Woody wanted the fans to know that this group of seniors was pretty special for the Ohio State during those four years that we played."

**Doug Plank shares an off the field experience that was his most memorable Buckeye moment:**

"You know what, I guess probably the biggest story that I ever had, really just brought a tear to my eye, was the Rose Bowl. It wasn't when I was playing, it was after 10 years or whatever. I moved out to Arizona and I was doing things out here and actually started working for Fox Sports Arizona doing broadcasting for Arizona State Games and University of Arizona football games.

"I became pretty close with some of those kids who were on that team. Jake Plummer was the quarterback. Pat Tillman was one of the defensive backs or that hyper linebacker position. Anyway, they go through and they win the Pac-12. Now, they're going to go to Rose Bowl to play Ohio State. My parents would never have had enough money to afford going to Rose Bowl. Since they would come out and stay with my wife and I for several months during the winter, I thought, "You know what, this would be an unbelievable experience for them to take them out to Rose Bowl.

"Which is what we did. That's the first time I ever saw a Rose Bowl parade, Tom. Man, that Rose Bowl parade is better than playing the game. I mean, that thing is like, you can't imagine. You just sit there and one unbelievable float after another comes driving by, and it was just stunning to see all the colors and just how majestic those things are. Of course, they take all year to build them. It isn't like it's a couple days event. We saw the parade and then went to the game. It was an unbelievable game. It was like one of those games of all times. Joe Germaine was the quarterback, and do you remember, he'd drive the ball down at the end of the game and score a touchdown. Then like USC in my senior year, which they beat us 18 to 17, they decide to go for two. A receiver by the name of Sheldon Diggs caught a two-point conversion and we lose 18 to 17. I know how bad that felt. Who would think years later, being at another game, with Ohio State, in the Rose Bowl. Doing exactly the same thing to Arizona State, that USC did to Ohio State. Which was the old, bend and break program. Where you're playing not to lose instead of playing to win. I've never found that philosophy to ever work as a player, or as a coach, but that's what we were doing that year. We were being more cautious, and playing over the top, and figure out how to score a touchdown and score two points. That's what Arizona State was doing to Ohio State. Joe Germaine just kept picking their defense apart all the way down.

"I'm trying to think Ohio State had that real large receiver at that time, David Boston. Big tall guy. He had an impact in the NFL too for a while when he first got drafted. He was their key receiver all year long. He's the one that caught the touchdown pass. I'm not exactly sure who got the two-point conversion, but that was an unbelievable game. You know what, and here's the one thing about it. Everybody's laughing and crying and cheering and all this kind of stuff. My parents were with us, and my mother was just crying like she'd just lost somebody in the family or something. I said, 'Are you okay?' Said, 'Mom, are you all right?' She was crying uncontrollably. She said, 'Doug, I just wish I could have been here for you when you played in this game.' Oh my God, tears running down her face. And I just said, 'You were here, you were in my heart even though you weren't here in the stadium,' and it was—sounds crazy, it was the most touching moment I had in my Ohio State career of having a moment that will live forever."

**As many Buckeyes do, Clark Kellogg struggled to identify only one greatest Buckeye memory:**

"It's tough for me to identify one single greatest moment, memory, experience of playing at Ohio State. Man, I don't know if I have a greatest. A lot of good memories around team and individual performance. I would probably say being part of that team in my freshman year in 1980, 1979, '80 with Herb, William, and Kelvin Ransey, and Jim Smith, Carter Scott; that was the best team I played on.

"We had a victory in a tournament against Arizona State, who also had a number of future NBA players on their roster. We actually beat them on their court. That was prior to the Field of 64 being the Field of 64. I think it was 48 teams at the time, and we got by and then there was still occasions where you might even play on somebody else's own floor. The sites weren't neutral. We actually had to go out to Tempe and play Arizona State on their court and beat them. That's one of my really proud memories as a Buckeye.

But beating Indiana in the end whenever we did, was always great. We only did that a couple of times, just because Bob Knight's relationship to the school and his place in the game as a hall of fame coach, a former Buckeye himself. Indiana teams being championship caliber pretty much throughout his time as the head coach there, particularly in the late '70s, early '80s. He actually won the championship in '81. Being able to perform well against them and beat them once in my freshman year. I made some free throws later to seal the win. And then we beat them again in my junior year in a game where I performed really well. Those are two Indiana games that stand out. The Arizona State victory in the tournament would probably be right up there too."

**Clark Clifton Kellogg, Jr.** is a former great Ohio State Buckeye Basketball Player, 1982 Big Ten Most valuable player, former player in the National Basketball Association (NBA) for the Indiana Pacers, former VP of player relations for the Indiana Pacers, the lead college basketball analyst for CBS Sports, and a current Member of The Ohio State University's board of trustees.

# Clark Kellogg

- Ohio State Basketball 1979-1982
- All Big ten – 1982
- Big Ten Most Valuable Player – 1982
- 1982 Drafted 1st Round – Indiana Pacers
- 1982 NBA All Rookie Team
- Lead College Basketball Analyst – CBS Sports
- Ohio State Board of Trustees – 2010-Present

*Garth Cox shares some memories from his freshman year that he will never forget:*

"I was a freshman and so all that excitement of Michigan week was all new to me and the people going crazy and the fans going nuts, and when you're trying to get off the field and that was mobbed with fans storming the field. We'd won on four field goals and I was playing on the field goal unit so I got to play, which was a goal of mine as a freshman, so, at least I got to contribute. But, that was crazy. That was probably one of the most memorable just because it was the first. Then we had other Michigan games we won up to the next year and stuff like that.

"But that one probably, because it was the first. My first trip to the Rose Bowl was as a freshman was just unbelievable. Because it was something I saw on TV, and you're sitting there, you're a freshman playing in front of 100,000 people and millions on TV. I remember trotting out on the field for the field goal and I was amazed by the sea of people in the stands.

"The other memory was the first time I ever went out of the tunnel at Ohio Stadium as a player, I remember looking up in the corner and there's more people in the stands than lives in my hometown. It was just crazy. Because we played like a noon or one o'clock back then. And we come out of the tunnel in September and it's just bright as it can be and all the colors. And I looked up and said there's more people there than live in my home town. That was the first thing that went through my head.

"Recently, we were joking about a story when we played at Michigan State my freshman year. We had a situation, I don't know if I know the story behind it, but the bottom line is, they weren't supposed to beat us, we were undefeated and all that. Near the end of the game we were down on goal line trying to score, time is running down and MSU is holding Steve Meyer, our center, down after the play to try & run out the clock. Meyer's trying to get up and they're holding him down by his face mask. Then finally we get up, we get the ball playing, the ball gets snapped, Champ Henson is handed the ball and fumbles, but Brian Baschnagle picks up the fumble and dives into the end-zone. Touchdown–we win!!! The refs leave the field in a hurry, and we're trying to get to the locker room through the mass of Michigan State fans that have swarmed the field.

"You know how that is, getting off the field when it is packed with people like that, but as we are running off, this guy sticks a camera right against Coach Hayes's nose and he halls off and he punches him. We made it to the locker room and then some forty-five minutes later, Wayne Duke, the Big Ten Commissioner comes in and says we've lost, and then Woody just really lost it. He went crazy. We go to our locker room and it was 45 minutes before Wayne Duke comes in and tells us that the score is not allowed, Michigan State wins. Coach Hayes goes ballistic, and they're trying to stop him from going after Wayne Duke. He wants a fight, and he's going crazy. Back then, my locker is beside Nick Buonamici because my number is 78, his is 75.

"Then Woody grabs Buonamici and he wants Nick to go out with him to go fight Wayne Duke, and everybody in the hallway, because he'd just taken the game or stole the game away from us. Nick holds back, but then we go out into the tunnel from the locker room and Woody has Wayne Duke pinned up against the wall! If that game were played today, with instant replay, we definitely would have won that game."

**Gene Smith, current Director of Athletics at Ohio State explains some of his best memories:**

"There's so many. It's so hard, because I care about every student-athlete we have. I was in Athens, Georgia, and we had Miho Kowase, and Francesca Di Lorenzo win the doubles national championship in women's tennis. Our women's tennis program never had a national championship, but our gold team was in the final four. I'm going to tell you, that was really cool watching our men's lacrosse team play in the national championship game in Gillette Stadium. We lost the national championship game, but we were there. We had a chance to win it. Those are recent memories, watching our volleyball team here on our campus. We hosted the volleyball national championship. We won the national championship. How rare is that when you bid to host the national championship three years in advance, and you win the opportunity to host it, and then your team can win in their own backyard. Those things are unbelievable.

"Then you got the national championship game in football. We beat Oregon, and it'd be hard for me to really say there's one, because there's so many. Then I have experiences here with young guys who I never thought would graduate. To watch Cardale Jones walk across that stage, remembering back to his freshman year, battling with him about going to class, not missing his tutors and trying to get to study table. You have guys like that on your team, and all along the way you're just worried, is he ever going to get it done? And here he comes back from his first year of playing with the Buffalo Bills, comes back and for a semester goes to school so he can graduate. I've had those proud moments. I'm going to tell you this because it's hard, it's hard for me to pick one because I have so many moments like that that were just beyond the competition, so phenomenal.

"Isn't that the one that started out the famous tweet of, 'I didn't come here to go to class, I came here to play football,' whatever he said, then he got killed, and here he was, he had 35 family members come to his graduation from Cleveland. It was hard for me to say this one thing sticks out, because there's just so many of them that were so special. We're blessed. We hosted the synchronized swimming national championships,. We won our 30th national championship in synchronized swimming. Man, I go down on deck with those girls and they're just trying to get me to jump into the pool. I didn't do it, but those moments.

"We had 200 synchronized swimming alumni back and I'm sitting with them, we're a having a great time watching our team win. I'm blessed in this job, it's just to see those special moments—it's amazing."

***Former Buckeye Quarterback and Big Ten Networks Sports Anchor, Stanley Jackson, has some great memories of his Buckeye Days:***

"We all have great football memories way back to Pop Warner. But for me, it was two things; let me say there's two moments, two separate years. The first one was when it's finally my job, when the coaches and the players acknowledged that I would be the starting quarterback. Some guys come in, and they get that as freshmen. Most of us have to wait a few years. Even when Bob Hoying graduated, I still had to fight for it. Joe and Tom (Germaine and Hoying) were there, and they brought in Mark Garcia. It was a fight. Everybody could play. Now, I was starter here at this place with the history and 100,000 fans in the stadium, it was significant. It was thrilling. I still remember those moments. I remember them fondly. That to me was just as good as it gets. It's hard to put those moments into words.

"My second, and this was a close second too. This is 1A and 1B. I would say it was. I was becoming a team captain my senior year. I know Urban designates captains now, but back then the players voted for the captains. The coaches didn't intervene, whoever the players voted for were the captains. I remember at the time John Cooper said I had received the most votes than any captain that he had ever had.

"It's significant when you get that position or any position you're a starter. Then you quickly learn that's when the real work starts. There's nothing like that. There's nothing like being acknowledged by—and not just the coaches but by your teammates, that you're the best guy for the job.

"That was a significant moment because that told me I turned the corner a little bit. I was maturing, and it was showing up. It was a level of leadership that I knew I had in me that was important to be acknowledged. Those were my moments. They weren't necessarily on the field moments. It was the off the field stuff that has a profound impact on my life even today."

## STANLEY JACKSON

- Ohio State Football 1994 – 1997
- Ohio State Quarterback 1994 – 1995
- Ohio State Starting Quarterback 1996
- 1997 Rose Bowl Champion
- Seattle Seahawks 1997
- Montreal Alouettes 1999-2000
- Toronto Argonauts 2001-2002
- Winnipeg Blue Bombers 2004
- Marion Mayhem 2007-2009
- BTN College Football Analyst – 2012-Present

**Matt Finkes has some terrific memories of his best experience as a Buckeye:**

"I think it's probably winning the Rose Bowl in '97, that being your last game, my senior year. We had so many seniors that we had been through a lot, obviously, with Coach Cooper, especially on the defense side. Myself, Mike and Luke, we'd been starting for three years on the defensive line and playing together for four years on the defensive line. Greg Bellisari, Ryan Miller, Shawn Springs, Rob Kelly and all those guys, that we'd been there for so long and had always fallen short of the goal, when you go back to '95, losing in the Michigan game when we came in undefeated and heavily favored with a team that was so good.

"With Eddy winning the Heisman, Terry winning the Beletnikoff Award, you had Bobby Hoying. It was a team that just had everything and just fell a little bit short. So, to finally get to the Rose Bowl and win it in 1997. I just remember, after that game, being in the locker room with guys and not wanting to take your pads off and not wanting to take your jersey off. Just sitting there and taking pictures with that Rose Bowl trophy and being happy that, obviously, you go out on a high note and you win the game. We didn't know it yet but at the time, we still thought we had a chance at the national title because everyone was going to have one loss that year.

"That and sitting around and also feeling the sadness to it, of that being the last game that you're never going to play for Ohio State, the last time you're going to put on that jersey. Like I said, just sitting there in the locker room with those guys. Yes, the celebrations and winning the game on the field was great, but honestly, being in the locker room after the game and just celebrating with the guys and taking that all in was probably the best experience I ever had.

"One of the best memories I have, and my regards to you, was the time that you took the fumble off that guy's back at Indiana and took it to the house. So, that was—

"Yes, that was a good one but I think the Rose Bowl is a little bit better in my mind."

## Matt Finkes

- Ohio State Football 1993 – 1996
- Ohio State Starting Defensive Lineman – 1995 – 1996
- 11 Sacks 1994
- Rose Bowl Champion – 1997
- 1997 6th Round draft pick – Carolina Panthers

*Jim Lachey, Former All-American Guard for the Buckeyes and former All Pro Offensive Tackle for the Washington Redskins shared some great thoughts.*

"I am so thankful that I had the opportunity to play in those Ohio State/Michigan games, Lachey said. "The fans and the intensity of the game were incredible. I later found out that if I could apply that same level of intensity from the Ohio State/Michigan game to the rest of my life; I would be great in life.

"When I played in the NFL, there were a lot of guys who had great experiences and who thought had played in big games, but they had played in NOTHING like the Ohio State/Michigan Game," he said. **Buckeyes for Life!**

## Jim Lachey

- *Ohio State Football 1981 – 1984*
- *First-team All-American 1984*
- *San Diego Chargers – 1985-1987*
- *Los Angeles Raiders – 1988*
- *Washington Redskins – 1988-1995*
- *Super Bowl champion (XXVI)*
- *3× Pro Bowl 1987, 1990, 1991*
- *3× AP First-team All-Pro 1989-1991*
- *AP Second-team All-Pro 1987*
- *70 Greatest Redskins*

**Keith Byars, former All-American Running Back for the Buckeyes remembers,**

"I've had a lot of great experiences in football; I've played in bowl games, a Pro Bowl and a Super Bowl, but that 1984 Illinois game was by far the greatest experience I've ever had!"

"Our line was the best offensive line I ever saw, college or NFL," Keith said. "We had John Frank, a great blocking tight end, Jim Lachey, William Roberts, Kirk Lowdermilk, and Mark Krerowicz, all who played in the NFL.

"I will never forget the look in their eyes during that last drive during that," Byars said. The game was tied 38-38 with

3:18 to go in the game and they said "We ain't playing for no tie!!" (The current NCAA overtime period began in 1996).

"It was vintage Ohio State Football," Keith said. "We knocked them off the ball and ran it down their throats. When we had the ball 3$^{rd}$ and goal at the Illinois 6-yard line, everybody in the stadium knew we were going to run the ball; the fans knew it, we knew it, Illinois knew it and they couldn't stop us. "I remember it like it was yesterday, Byars said. **Buckeyes for Life!**

Brian Baschnagel was one of the great players and icons of the 1970s glory years of Ohio State Football. Baschnagel became the team captain of the 1974 Big Ten Champion Ohio State Buckeyes. He played in four Rose Bowls, was drafted by the Chicago Bears, and enjoyed a successful 10 year NFL career

**When talking with Brian about the greatest experiences he had in all of those great football playing days, Brian was quick to identify two experiences that linked with each other:**

"I will never forget the intensity of the 1973 Ohio State/Michigan game when we tied 10 to 10. It was such an incredibly tense game in the greatest rivalry in college football," Baschnagel said. "We then went on to the Rose Bowl and demolished a USC team that included Anthony Davis, Ricky Bell, Pat Haden, Gary Jeter, Jim Obradovich, and Lynn Swann. It was one of the greatest times of my life!"

Baschnagel had a great Ohio State career during an absolute golden period of Buckeye football. During that time, the Buckeyes record was 40-5-1 and they won four straight Big Ten Championships, played in four Rose Bowls and finished #3 in 1972, #2 in 1973, #3 in 1974 and #4 in 1975.

Brian then went on to play 10 years with the Chicago Bears with things coming "full circle" from his recruiting days with Woody Hayes.

**Maurice Hall has some wonderful memories from his days as a Buckeye:**

"There's actually two, man. One being, obviously, scoring the winning touchdown against Michigan in the game that got us to the national championship. There's nothing like playing in that game. For one, being able to play and having an opportunity to make a play that helped to beat them and then also helped send us to 13 - 0 and go to the national championship. I'll never forget that experience; the loudness of the stadium, how much of a high we were on as a team during that time. "The other one is the opportunity as well in the stadium to get my college degree. My parents didn't go to college. Growing up, I didn't have any role models in my family. My parents didn't go to college, their brothers and sisters didn't go to college, so I never had a real role model, seeing someone go to college and actually graduate," Maurice said. "So being able to do that, especially with my parents being there and watching me, and being that happy, was very emotional and was a big accomplishment for me as a person, as a family man. I want to be an example for my two girls that are going to be growing older and need someone to set a different example that my parents weren't able to do. So, I would say those are my two greatest experiences." ***"Buckeyes for Life"***

## Maurice Hall

- Ohio State Football 2001 – 2004
- Scored winning touchdown in 2001 Michigan Game
- 2002 National Championship
- 2002 Fiesta Bowl, 2003 Fiesta Bowl, 2004 Alamo Bowl, 2005 Fiesta Bowl

**All-time great Buckeye and NFL Hall of Fame receiver, Chris Carter shares his best experience as a Buckeye:**

"My greatest experience at Ohio State was probably with the older players, Mike Tomczak, Jim Lachey, Keith Byars and Pepper Johnson, former Ohio State All-American receiver and NFL Hall of Fame member," Chris Carter said. "Those guys really took care of me when I was a freshman. They helped me transition from high school, not only in football, but off the field. I appreciated how much they cared about me and they helped get my career off on the right path.

"The other great experience at Ohio State I had was with Coach Tressel while he was an assistant coach at Ohio State," Carter said. "He more than any of the other coaches or people in the administration stayed close to me since I left Ohio State. He and I had a great relationship and we have stayed close ever since."

## Chris Carter

- Ohio State Football 1984 – 1986
- Ohio State Starting Receiver 1984 – 1986
- Consensus All American – 1986
- Ohio State Buckeyes MVP 1986
- Philadelphia Eagles 1987-1989
- Minnesota Vikings 1990-2001
- Miami Dolphins 2002
- 8× Pro Bowl 1993-2000
- 2× First-team All-Pro 1994, 1999
- Second-team All-Pro 1995
- Walter Payton NFL Man of the Year 1999
- 3× NFL receiving touchdowns leader 1995, 1997, 1999
- NFL 1990s All-Decade Team
- Minnesota Vikings No. 80 retired
- Minnesota Vikings Ring of Honor
- NFL Hall of Fame – 2015

**Pete Cusick was inducted into the Ohio State Athletics Hall of Fame class of 2012. While speaking with Pete recently, the Hall of Fame induction was still fresh in his mind and a huge sense of pride for him.**

"The Hall of Fame was a tremendous honor," Cusick said. "It was one of the greatest moments of my life and I am still on cloud nine! It was a great compliment to my Ohio State career, but also an honor to be in the same class with people like Mike Vrabel, Ray Griffin, Jessica Davenport, and Dick Schafrath."

Despite all the accolades and being a member of a team that went 29-4-1 over three years, Cusick remains humble about his career at Ohio State.

Cusick was a 1974 All-American, team captain, played in three Rose Bowls, and played for the New England Patriots in the NFL. "Given all that, the greatest experience I had at Ohio State was absolutely playing for Woody Hayes," Cusick said. "I loved the way he was all business and coached us to play great defense. Woody also taught us to 'Pay Forward' to other people. It has always come back to me in spades 20-30 years later. I became successful inherently from being a part of the Ohio State Program. No gray area. It made me the best in the business world.

"The other great memory of my Ohio State playing days were playing every year in the Ohio State/Michigan Game and going on to play in the Rose Bowl," Cusick said. "You come to Ohio State to win the big games. We did and it was awesome! "At Ohio State, it's about the tradition, the excellence, the winning, and the respect. Winning the right way. We come back year after year and we do it again. I am so proud of Ohio State," Pete said.

The evening when Pete was inducted into the Hall of fame, he closed by saying, "I love this place, I love all of you and thank you, it's been wonderful!" It sure has Pete! **Buckeyes for Life!**

## Pete Cusick

- Ohio State Football 1971 – 1974
- Starting Defensive tackle 1972 – 1974
- Consensus All American 1974
- New England Patriots 1975
- Television Advertising's Marlboro Man

**Eddie George shared his most memorable experience:**

"It is such an honor and privilege to be able to work for Ohio State, which gave me so much and helped me grow personally and professionally," George said in a news release. "I am grateful to have the opportunity to apply what I've learned from my academic and football journey while at the university, along with the work I've been doing in the world of business, to support the transformative initiatives happening at my alma mater."

Having had such tremendous experiences and successes on the field, one might be surprised at George's greatest experience in football. "I had so many great experiences at Ohio State," George said. "But the greatest experience had to be putting on that scarlet and gray jersey for the first time. Walking into the stadium on game day for the first time. It was real, it was visceral, it was tangible and you could taste the energy in the stadium. You could smell the grass and hear roar of the crowd.

I dreamed about it as a child. To walk in there wearing that uniform to represent the scarlet and gray was awesome. And although I didn't play a lot that day, I relished the opportunity to cheer on my teammates."

As Assistant Vice President and as an ambassador for the Ohio State University, Eddie George will continue cheering on his teammates. You're a great Buckeye, Eddie. We will keep cheering you on as well.

## EDDIE GEORGE

- Ohio State Football 1984 – 1986
- Ohio State Starting Receiver 1984 – 1986
- Heisman Trophy – 1995
- Walter Camp Award – 1995
- Maxwell Award – 1995
- Doak Walker Award – 1995
- Consensus All-American – 1995
- Ohio State Buckeyes No. 27 retired
- Tennessee Titans – 1996-2003
- Dallas Cowboys – 2004
- 4× Pro Bowl – 1997-2000
- First-team All-Pro – 2000
- Second-team All-Pro – 1999
- NFL Offensive Rookie of the Year – 1996

**Tim Spencer, former All Big Ten running back for The Ohio State Buckeyes was one of our best players ever. Spencer coached nine years for the Chicago Bears and is now entering into his fifth season as the running back coach for the Tampa Bay Buccaneers. He was a four-year letterman at Ohio State, a two-year starter and still ranks third in all-time rushing yards with 3,553 yards.**

I will personally never forget the 1979 Michigan game in Ann Arbor in a season that very closely parallels this 2012 season. We were striving to finish the year with an undefeated record, just like our 2012 Buckeyes are trying to do. That day in Michigan Stadium in front of 105,000 fans, we were clinging to an 18-15 lead with 3:50 to play and I'll never forget Tim, rumbling for first down after first down as a true freshman, helping ice the victory, an undefeated season, a Big Ten Championship, and a trip to the Rose Bowl.

Spencer played and coached for the Buckeyes, played for the San Diego Chargers, and has been the running backs coach for the Chicago Bears for the last nine years. He is no stranger to tremendous football experiences. "Coaching in the Super Bowl with the Bears and coaching in the 2002 National Championship game were two of my greatest experiences, but playing in the 1979 Michigan game and the Rose Bowl for Ohio State was the greatest experience ever," Spencer said.

After that Rose Bowl, Tim went on to play in the Fiesta Bowl, Liberty Bowl, and the Holiday Bowl, where he led the Buckeyes with 167 yards rushing on our way to defeating the BYU Cougars 47-17.

Since then, Tim has stayed active since his playing and coaching days with Ohio State and has never stopped following the Buckeyes. "I've continued to follow them ever since I played," Spencer said. We have practice every Saturday morning with the Bears, so I tape the game and usually get home to start watching right after the first quarter. I wouldn't miss it for the world!"

## TIM SPENCER

- Ohio State Football 1979 – 1982
- First-team All-Big Ten – 1982
- Ohio State Most Valuable Player – 1982
- Fourth on OSU's all-time rushing list – 3,553 yards
- Chicago Bears Running Back Coach – 2004 – 2012
- Tampa Bay Buccaneers Running Back Coach – 2014-Present

**Paul Warfield is one of the Greatest Buckeyes of all time. Warfield played halfback for the Buckeyes from 1960 – 1963 and went on to a great career with the Cleveland Browns and Miami Dolphins of the NFL. While playing in the NFL, Paul was named all pro six times, played in three Super Bowls, eight Pro Bowls and was the starting wide receiver for the only undefeated team in National Football League history, the 1976 Miami Dolphins.**

"One of the proudest moments I had as a Buckeye was when we won the 1961 Big Ten Championship," Warfield said. "We had worked so hard, going undefeated and we beat Michigan 50 to 20 in Ann Arbor.

"It was also one of my biggest disappointments as the Ohio State board of trustees voted that football was infringing on our educational experience and then declined our invitation to participate in the 1962 Rose Bowl. That would NEVER happen today, NEVER!" Warfield said

Minnesota went on to represent the Big Ten in the Rose Bowl, where they defeated UCLA 21-3. Despite not being able to compete in the Rose Bowl, Ohio State was still recognized as a National Champion by one of the polls, the FWAA (Football Writers Association of America), giving the Buckeyes a split title.

Warfield, having played 14 years in the NFL, including his six all pro seasons and three Super Bowls, has some extraordinary experiences and memories of a lifetime, but he indicated two that stood out above the rest: Being a member of the 1976 Undefeated Miami Dolphins and the 50th anniversary and reunion of the Ohio State 1961 National Championship Team.

"Walking out on that field again, in that awesome Ohio Stadium, in front of 108,000 fans for the Wisconsin game was just incredible!" Warfield said. "The hair went up on the back of my neck; I got a tear in my eye and chills down my spine. It reminded me what a great institution the Ohio State University is and what a great experience it was to be an Ohio State Buckeye!"

As a reminder to Buckeye fans, there were some very special people that Warfield had as team mates and coaches of that 1961 team. Some of the most notable are as follows: Bob Ferguson – fullback; Minnesota Vikings Gary Moeller-Linebacker/Center; Head Coach, University of Michigan, Matt Snell – half back; New York Jets Bob Vogel – tackle; Baltimore Colts John Havlicek – wide receiver; Cleveland Browns, Boston Celtics and member of the NBA Hall of Fame, Bo Schembechler – assistant coach, head coach at the University of Michigan; and the one and only Woody Hayes as the head coach.

"It was an awesome group of people, Warfield said. "But most of all, I wish Woody could have been at the reunion. He was like a father to me. Yes, he was tough, but he taught me the importance of education, character, discipline, hard work, integrity, and honesty. He made me who I am today. I will never forget him slapping me on the back and how happy he was when I received my master's degree in 1977. Woody was all about the educational experience. My experiences at Ohio State were the greatest of my life and it is truly great to be an Ohio State Buckeye!" ***Buckeyes for Life!***

## PAUL WARFIELD

- Ohio State Football 1960 – 1963
- Ohio State Starting Halfback 1962, 1963
- National champion – 1961
- 2× First-team All-Big Ten – 1962, 1963
- Cleveland Browns – 1964-1969
- Miami Dolphins – 1970-1974
- Memphis Southmen – 1975
- Cleveland Browns – 1976-1977
- Miami 2× Super Bowl champion VII, VIII
- Cleveland Browns NFL champion – 1964
- 8× Pro Bowl – 1964, 1968-1974
- 6× First-team All-Pro – 1964, 68, 69, 1971-73

- Second-team All-Pro – 1970
- 2× NFL receiving touchdowns leader – 1968, 1971
- NFL 1970s All-Decade Team

**Teresa Fightmaster, one of the greatest women swimmers in the history of The Ohio State University shared her most memorable experiences as one of the "Swimmin Women" at Ohio State:**

"It would probably be the 1983 Big Ten Swimming Championships. That was the second year. My freshman year was our second year that Ohio State had won it consecutively. At that meet we had—I don't remember how many, but we had multiple Big Ten Champions. I think I won three events there. As a freshman, that was pretty exciting individual events, plus we had won relays. We just crushed the opponents. I just thought, 'Man, life is good.' It was an amazing experience. Everybody was on cloud nine. Ohio State just—it was one of those meets that it just seemed like it was surreal. I'll never forget it!

"Another great experience was my induction into the Ohio State Athletics Hall of Fame. It came years after the Mirror Lake Incident where a girl was pushed in to Mirror Lake, she was a swimmer and she ended up being a quadriplegic. That was a swimmer. That was Coach Jim and Bev Montrella's daughter.

"It was in the fall of '85, November, and long story short, that was my senior year and that was one of the toughest years that we had with just the coaches, the swimmers. It was life altering. I was just- yes, one of the toughest things. That was the year, I think, we only won the Big Ten, I think by less than five points, but we did it for her and it was just incredible. It was so hard. She passed away, I think, four years ago.

"That was one of those big experiences I think that put a lot of things in perspective for all. How short life is, but how important friendships are. That was huge. She was back for my Ohio State Athletics Hall of Fame induction in 2002 and Jim inducted me. That was during the time that you'd had somebody induct you versus you going out there.

"I think that really the coolest thing about that was not only being a part of the Ohio State Athletics Hall of Fame, but walking out during like a football game and standing there and waving, and then hearing later that my former swimmers and teammates and just friends were there, and just to be so proud. My grandma was still alive to experience that. That was probably one of the biggest thrills that I've had my life so far. That was pretty a neat thrill." *"BUCKEYES for Life"*

As a kid, growing up, I had the pleasure and privilege to become indoctrinated to college football by watching my brother play at the University of Illinois. I was fortunate at that time because from the age of 12 to 14, I was able to watch the "U of I" play teams and players such as the Washington Huskies – with "Sonny Sixkiller," Penn State with John Capelletti, Michigan State with Brad VanPelt, Southern Cal with Lynn Swann, Pat Hayden and Sam "The Bam" Cunningham, Michigan with Gordon Bell and Rob Lytle and The Ohio State University with Archie Griffin, Cornelius Green, Randy Gradishar, Nick Buonamici, and Tim Fox. Tim Fox became a three time All-American at strong safety and was one of two players in history to start in the Rose Bowl for four years. The other was none other than Archie Griffin. Not a bad early exposure to college football for a young teenager!

One of the most memorable games I witnessed was Ohio State at Illinois in 1975. My brother was team captain for Illinois and had worked all off season and pre-season with this game in his sights.

Tim Fox, was one of the key players of that 1975 game.

I will never forget that game. Uncharacteristically, the Buckeyes came out slow, trading field goals with the Illini during the first quarter, with Illinois field goal kicker, Dan Beaver, kicking a 53-yard field goal to put Illinois ahead 3 to 0. The second quarter was just as lackluster with the only highlight being Archie Griffin's 30-yard touchdown run. Before the half, with time running down, the Buckeyes were marching on a late drive. Time was running down, when Woody sent in kicker Tom Skladany, who boomed a 59-yard field goal to put the Buckeyes ahead 10 to 3. It was one of those "In Your Face" moments.

As the second half began, Illinois had the ball and quarterback Jim Kopatz faded back to pass. He threw a long pass out near the 50-yard line that was intercepted by none other than Tim Fox. Fox returned the interception 50 yards for a touchdown, doing a head over heels front flip, never breaking stride as he crossed the goal line. The score was now Ohio State 17 – Illinois 3. The message had been sent and certainly delivered. Final score Ohio State 40 – Illinois 3.

Woody Hayes was always known for despising end zone celebrations. He used to urge players to hand the ball to the referee and celebrate with your teammates on the sideline. Woody used to say, "Act like you've been there before."

In 1975, QB Cornelius Greene scored many touchdowns running the option play, culminating with an end zone shuffle that always irritated Woody.

When talking with Fox, I asked him how Coach Hayes reacted to his full front flip as he crossed the goal line against the Illini. Tim said that Woody was not too pleased, but that in the post-game film review sessions, Woody said, "Fox, you know I hate end zone celebrations, but that was one hell of an athletic move, son."

Larry Romanoff, former Director of External Relations for Ohio State Football, once told me the story of Fox at the 1976 Rose Bowl, doing flips off of the bridge of the Huntington Sheraton Hotel into the pool. Woody was again incensed.

Tim Fox was one of the greatest safeties to ever play for the Buckeyes. He played in four Rose Bowls, was a two-time

All American and was drafted in the first round by the New England Patriots. He played 14 years in the NFL for the New England Patriots, San Diego Chargers and the L.A. Rams. Having earned all those accolades and accomplishments, I asked Fox to share his greatest memory of his football playing days. Tim was quick to point out two memories.

"One was being drafted in the first round of the NFL Draft by the New England Patriots. I had no expectations of being drafted anywhere near the first round," Fox said

"I wasn't even home that day; I was out shopping and hanging out with some friends. They broke the news to me when I got home. That was a terrific memory and I went on to have a really good NFL career," he said.

The other memory Fox had was one of his greatest losses. "When I speak to young kids and youth organizations today, I always tell them you learn more from the losses than the wins," Tim said. I will never forget our 1975 Rose Bowl loss to UCLA. We had already beaten them by 21 points earlier in the year and then lost to them 23 to 10 in the Rose Bowl. I could have played better and we all could have played better and we would have won the national Championship. I think about it to this day, and it has helped me persevere and succeed in life.

"Despite that, I have great memories of Ohio State," Fox said. "We only lost five games in four years and we were one of the winningest classes in Ohio State History."

## Tim Fox

- Ohio State Football 1972 – 1975
- Four Year Starter – Strong Safety
- Team Captain – 1975
- Consensus 1st team All American – 1975
- New England Patriots – 1976-1981
- San Diego Chargers – 1982 – 1984
- Los Angeles Rams – 1985-1986
- Pro Bowl (1980)
- New England Patriots All-1970s Team

**Ernie Andria talks some more about our great Buckeye Brotherhood:**

"I have so many, I have so many good memories. All my memories of playing football I would do over again tomorrow. I mean all of them.

"My best playing memory is from the Rose Bowl against USC in 1980. Even though we were the number one ranked team in the country, we were really, really big underdogs. And even though we lost that game, we probably played just about as good as we could play, I think. And when you consider the fact that they had two, not one, but two Heisman Trophy winners on the playing field, Charles White and Marcus Allen.

"They probably had the best offensive line the NFL has ever seen and the big dog, Anthony Munoz, who is now enshrined in the NFL Hall of Fame. And that was the only game he played in that year! He was injured for most of the season and gave up a redshirt year to come back and play against us in the Rose Bowl. But man, they had Keith Vanhorn at right tackle. They had Brad Buddy at guard. They had Chris Foote at center. They were unbelievable.

"It was just an amazing, an amazing game and it was so— we were playing so well that day. I mean, I don't remember much about football games, really. I can't break down, I can't go to a game and then tell you all the plays. But for that game for some reason, I just remember so much of the actual game. All the things that went on. Their defensive then was the number one. They had guys like Joey Browner and Ronnie Lott and they had the number one outside defensive end of football, Chip Banks. Chip Banks. I blocked him. And I beat his ass all day. long. I was hooking him, I was doing everything to him. I just didn't have much of a problem with Chip Banks that day. I had a good game actually and that's probably my highlight from a football standpoint. That USC team was one of the most talented teams in the history of college football and we lost in the final seconds 17 to 16, you know what I mean?

"You know we had 24 guys in our 1976 recruiting class," Ernie said. "And most of us are all going to Treasure Island, Florida for the fifth year in a row. Five years, it's been five years now. We all go to Joe Hornik's house for the weekend. We stay on the St. Pete Beach. Some of us get hotels. I actually stay at Joe's and we all go down there for Thursday, Friday, Saturday. Fly back on Sunday. And it's just growing every year. I think there might be 15 of us this year, you know what I mean.

"Next year I know Mark Sullivan, big Sully is going. It's just we all go to Joe's house. They have a big catering thing and everybody will go golfing or I'll go fishing. It's just wonderful. We just sit there and tell stories. Joe Hornik will be there,

Marty Cusick, Savoca, Burke, me, all our wives. It's just amazing. It's just how it is. It's great. **Buckeyes for Life** for sure."

**Tom Levenick: "I have written about my extensive "Big Ten Background" and while this personal experience is a departure from all my extraordinary "Buckeye Experiences," it may still be inspirational to many of you.**

I will never forget as a freshman in high school, traveling with my parents up to Madison, Wisconsin to watch my brother as the Team Captain of the Fighting Illini play against the Wisconsin Badgers. As I mentioned before, my uncle and cousin both played for the Badgers, and all of my relatives were from Madison. After my Uncle, Norris Ace finished his playing days for Wisconsin, he gave my grandparents his two season tickets each year.

That year as we were settling in to watch the Illini and Badgers play, my brother and Lonnie Perrin, the two Illinois Team Captains were at the 50-yard line for the coin toss with the Wisconsin captains Billy Marek and Dennis Lick. My mother, father, and I were seated on the west side of the stadium and my grandparents, Burdette and Eleanor Ace, were seated at the 50-yard line on the east side right in the middle of the "W" which was imprinted on the bleacher seats. Unbelievably and coincidently, just as they were doing the coin toss, the Wisconsin announcer came over the loud speaker, asking the Wisconsin fans to honor my grandparents for being season ticket holders for 25 straight years. They stood and the crowd gave them an ovation, right at the same time that their grandson was at the 50-yard line participating in the coin toss for the game. I looked at my mother and she was crying her eyes out. It was a very moving moment for all.

**Former Buckeye Assistant Coach and Hall of Fame Head coach at Notre Dame, Lou Holtz had great experiences as an assistant coach at Ohio State:**

"The highlight of my time at Ohio State would have been the third game of the year in 1968," Holtz said. "We started 16 sophomores and we're playing Purdue. They were number one in the country at the time. Mike Phipps was their quarterback. They had Leroy Keys at tailback and Jim Barney at center. They had beaten Ohio State the year before. Coach Hayes clearly let me know that I was hired for the Purdue game, so to speak. They came in number one in the country and we shut them out 13 - 0. After that game, the players all became real believers and eventually we beat Southern California and OJ Simpson in the Rose Bowl for the National Championship."

*Rex Kern is one of the all-time great Ohio State football players, who quarterbacked the Buckeyes during the 1968, 1970 and 1971 seasons. He was team captain and All-American quarterback of the 1968 National Championship team. The Buckeyes were 27-2 during Kerns tenure and defeated the O.J. Simpson led USC Trojans in the 1969 Rose Bowl.*

Obviously, Kern delivered us all some memories of a lifetime and experienced many himself. When I asked Rex about his greatest experiences in all of football, he told me "Without question, I was proud to earn three degrees from Ohio State. But it was the opportunity to make friends with all my teammates; the opportunity to play with those guys, every one of them. I have learned so much from them through the victories and the two adversities that we had. I have lifetime friends of my teammates and to know if I ever needed anything, they'd be there. It was incredible to play for Ohio

State, and a guy like Woody and the relationships were the most important thing."

***Like many Buckeyes, Tom Skladany's most memorable moment came from one of the Ohio State/Michigan games:***

"My best memory is in the 74 Michigan game in the 3rd qtr. when I had to punt from 8 yards deep in our end zone with the score 9-7 with us up and I knew I needed to bang one ... I handled the snap, and even though everyone was screaming ... I heard nothing and felt like I was moving in slow motion and thought my punt was going to be blocked, but lo and behold I hit my best punt of the year around 62 yards and got them the hell out of our side of the field ... everyone was smacking me on the helmet when I returned to the bench and it was then when I realized what I had done ... awesome feeling ... great memory."

# 10

## "WHAT ABOUT BOB?"

### (Who is your Bob Fenton?)

### (Who was that one person in their life, that went out of their way to help, develop and ensure future success for Former Buckeye Football Players?)

I recently spoke with Archie Griffin regarding the philosophy of "Paying Forward" that we were taught constantly by Coach Woody Hayes. While I personally learned that from my days at TOSU as you have read in my previous writing, I had an individual in my life, who also taught me how to go out of my way for other people, extend yourself, and "Pay Forward." After my days at Ohio State, I was a young man, with a young family, working as hard as I could every day, for 7-UP at the time and this gentleman seemed to go out of his way every day for me, unbeknownst to me and unsolicited by me. I would come home from work and my lawn would be mowed, or my car would be washed and if I had plumbing or electricity problems, he would come to help and sometimes stay past midnight until problems were solved. His name is Bob Fenton.

I bought a new home and moved about ten miles north of Columbus and many days, Bob would knock at the door at 6:00 a.m., asking if there was anything with which he could help me.

**Archie Griffin shared the "Bob Fenton" in his life:**

"Without question, the person who influenced my life the most, was my guidance counselor in Junior High School, Oscar Gill", Archie said. "I was on the student council and Oscar was my advisor. He taught us to be the best person you can be each and every day and to give it your best shot. He preached the three D's: **D**esire, **D**edication and **D**etermination. It has stuck with me every day," said Griffin. "And ever since that time, I have tried to apply it to every phase of my life. Oscar is **my** Bob Fenton."

Archie has gone on to become a timeless, uncompromising ambassador for The Ohio State University, as the CEO and now Senior Advisor for Advancement for the Ohio State Alumni Association. He is also the spokesman for the Wendy's High School Heisman Awards program; he is on the Board of Directors for Motorist Insurance, the National Football Foundation, and the College Football Hall of Fame.

Obviously, the three D's have not only helped Archie, he exemplifies those traits

He is an icon for the Ohio State University, an icon for Ohio State Football and an icon for our youth to admire and emulate as they grow, learn, and develop. **Buckeyes for Life!**

**Chris Spielman Shares the "Bob Fenton" in his life:**

"There were so many people that helped me; parents, teachers, coaches," Chris said. "But unquestionably, the person who went out of their way and helped me the most was my roommate, Frank Hoak. (Hoak played for the Buckeyes in

1984 to 1987.) When I was in school, I didn't have any money. Frank had a car and an allowance from his dad. We would go to Wendy's and he would always buy. He would let me use his car, even when he had his own plans. He would walk, but let me use his car. I will never forget all the great things Frank did for me. Chris and Frank remain close as Frank resides in Columbus, working for Nationwide Insurance."

Spielman obviously learned from Frank Hoak as he advanced through life and continued to do things for others, specifically through the Stephanie Spielman Foundation.

Spielman has grown from those days and has become a "Bob Fenton" who consistently "Pays Forward." As most of you know, the Stephanie Spielman Foundation was created in honor of Chris's late wife, who passed away due to breast cancer in 2009. The foundation continues today as a centerpiece of the Spielman family, raising funds for cancer research in conjunction with the American Cancer Society and the Arthur G. James Cancer Institute at The Ohio State University.

Thus far, the Stephanie Spielman Foundation has raised over $10,000,000 for cancer research through fund raising activities such as the Buckeye Cruise for cancer, The Step Up for Stephanie 5K walk/Run and the Bottomless Mug of Coffee, sponsored by Panera Bread Company.

Chris was proud to tell me that his daughter, Madison, and son, Noah, are both involved with the foundation; Madison helping out with public check presentations and Noah was the family representative on the most recent Buckeye Cruise for Cancer.

"I am really proud of them," Chris said. "I know their involvement keeps it fresh in their minds as to who and what Stephanie was."

Chris Spielman will go down as a legend in the history of Ohio State Football. What needs to be said and is readily evident is that Chris Spielman is also a terrific man, father, community leader and without question, he is a Buckeye for Life.

**Clark Kellogg also, like many other Buckeyes, especially including myself, had a "Bob Fenton" in his life:**

"Man, I tell you, I've had a number of folks step into that role, but probably the one that would rise to the top is a guy by the name of Ira Novak, Buckeye graduate, successful insurance agent for decades. I actually worked for him from the time I was a junior in high school during the summer until I went to the NBA in 1982. We've maintained a good, close friendship all of this time. But I would have to say he would be that type of person in my life, the guy who befriended me, took an interest in me, and has helped me journey successfully through each stage of my life, particularly, in relationship to business and dealing with people. But, no, he's been a tremendous mentor and friend for me over the years."

**Pepper Johnson had a very special "Bob Fenton" in his life:**

Well, my alumnus, Ronald Granaper. He's alumni bro of Ohio State. My mother and father separated when I was five years old. He took me under his wing and became a father figure. I call him my father today.

**Rick Bay shares a story about his "Bob Fenton:"**

"Gosh, well, I'll tell you, one guy. I couldn't name someone that did that covering a long span. I had certain individuals that helped me along the way at various times. Bo Schembechler was one of them. I would have never become the Athletic Director of Oregon without Bo and, therefore, transferred to Ohio State if it hadn't been for Bo. Because when I coached wrestling at Michigan, I didn't get along with the Athletic Director at the time, a guy named Don Canham. Even though I was a very successful coach, we just did not hit it off.

"When I was trying to get the job at Oregon then, I knew that Don would not give me a strong recommendation. I had to go to Bo and ask him to say something to Rich Brooks, the Oregon coach at the time, to counteract what I knew was probably coming from Mr. Canham. He did it even though Canham was his boss too. He did call Rich Brooks and that turned the tide. I was a very unexperienced guy in athletic administration. In fact, I had no experience in athletic administration and Oregon still hired me. That was the catapult to my career in becoming a sports executive at various levels."

**Buckeye Women's Basketball Great, Katie Smith has had many "Bob Fentons" in her life.**

"I've had a lot of champions for me whether it was high school or college, and even the pros, whether it was a teacher or coach or just a mentor," Smith said. I tell you what, it was too many personally to name. Barbara Fergus, she sponsored my scholarship at Ohio State and has over the years become a friend and mentor. Just behind the scenes, always with advice or just listening and just to have a plethora of knowledge in her world and always giving back and help try to pull, especially woman along and give them opportunities.

"I also wanted to say, Larry Romanoff and Kate Riffee were also two people who were impactful throughout my Ohio State and pro years. Honestly, even now I stay connected with them and have always leaned on them a little bit as mentors throughout all this. It's funny how people become lifelong friends.

"There are so many. Too many to really name *ONE* throughout my years, whether it was from my hometown to college, to pros, and continually do even to this day and people I don't even know about. Personally, I hope I've been good to them as much as they've been good to me. I'm sure there's been so many behind the scenes that have championed for me over the years."

**Current All American Buckeye Defensive End, Nick Bosa has a Great Bob Fenton, who has taken personal interest in him since he enrolled at Ohio State in 2016.**

"I'd probably go with Coach J, honestly, Coach Larry Johnson (Ohio State Defensive Line Coach). He loves you as a person and not just a player," Bosa said. "He's gone out of his way to check up on me whenever times are going hard or whenever it is, not just the coaching. It's more of just family. This year, he asked me over for Thanksgiving and Christmas dinner when my family couldn't make it up from Florida. Just having him here in Ohio where I'm far away from my family. He is a father figure away from home and it is great to have a position coach like that."

**Another former great Buckeye, Eddie George had a "Bob Fenton" in his life helping him along the way. Eddie George, as can be expected, was profound with his answer.**

"It is my wife Tamara," George said. "That's why I married her. She has been in my corner since the day I met her. I cannot say enough about her unwavering support. She not only wanted to be with me because she loved me, but also to help me reach my full potential as a father, as a husband, and as a man." She was obviously successful Eddie as you are that great father and husband and you are a terrific ambassador for The Ohio State University. **Buckeyes for Life!**

*A.J. Hawk had some significant appreciation for the "Bob Fenton" in his life and that appreciation is mutual.*

"My parents were obviously very important in my growth and development," A.J. said. "But one person who went out of his way and still does to this day is Jim Tressel. Coach Tressel helped me with football, my education, work ethic, and more than anything, he helped me with everyday life. He still does to this day. We talk almost every week and I have now been gone from Ohio State going on twelve years. Coach Tress was a great coach, but also a great leader and a great man. I am proud to have played for him and proud to call him my friend," Hawk said.

Aaron James Hawk...Nicknamed "A.J." by his parents since birth, after legendary Indy car driver A.J. Foyt, has an incredible work ethic. "He's amazing. All he does is work. He loves it, loves practice, loves the weight room, loves to hit people. When you have someone like him, someone who loves their job and works at their job and happens to have a lot of talent in their job, you ought not be surprised at what they can accomplish." *Former Ohio State Head Coach, Jim Tressel*

### Roy Hall talks about the "Bob Fenton" in his life:

"His name is Tom Rhodey. Tom Rhodey is the lead on campus currently for the Fellowship of Christian Athletes. He does a great job as a chaplain for the Ohio State football team, and a few other athletic teams at Ohio State. He's one of our team chaplains, and he's the guy that leads the bible studies, and gives the lessons, and meets with you one on one for 15 minutes once a week.

"He's a guy that introduced me to Christ, to Jesus Christ, and my faith. Everything that I am today, from a faith standpoint, was seeded by Tom Rhodey. For about three to four months, I really avoided Tom, and avoided the spiritual component, that faith conversation, that God conversation. Here you got an older white guy, he's probably in his 60s now, but when I was there, he was probably early 50s or whatever it may be. He has two hearing aids, you look at him, and he's walking around with his Bible, and always around, and trying to talk to other guys. And you are just like, 'Man, I really don't feel like hearing this.' When you're a younger guy, you really don't want to have that conversation because you're insecure. You don't really have the confidence to do it, or you have whatever assumptions or thoughts that you have about the Gospel, and God, and different things. He was a guy that didn't take no for an answer. What I mean by that, is I gave him every excuse in the book to not to talk to him, and he was always polite to me. Didn't really push me, but when he would see me, he would ask about how I was doing. How was my journey as a student athlete, if I need anything, if I wanted to go out for dinner, or lunch, to just offer his insight.

"Just a really polite man, and finally, I took the opportunity to get a chance to know him, other than just being passive and not speaking to him. It obviously led to a conversation on the gospel, and him just answering some questions for me, and just being open, and I was able to be honest, and he's one of my best friends today.

"I really owe him the world for that, because he took a chance on me continuously when he could've given up. 'Oh, this guy don't want to hear about what I'm talking about,' or, 'Didn't want to hear my message or hear God's message and left it alone,' but he really kept the door open and put me in a position to make that decision for myself, and now I have a base and foundation that's unshakeable. It's a foundation that allows me to do everything that I'm doing today with the Driven Foundation. It prevents me from being worried or being discouraged because I know God has my back and he's positioned me to be successful, and those are the things that allow me to serve him and why I have the attitude that I have right now. Tom Rhodey is my Bob Fenton, hands down. He's not a coach, He's the person that introduced me to Jesus and I owe him the world for that." ***"Buckeyes for Life".***

# Robert "Bob" Fenton

# 11

# "BUCKEYES FOR LIFE"

## (Why is the Bond of Former Ohio State Football Players so Strong?)

The bond of former Buckeye football players or "Buckeye Brotherhood" as we call it is truly amazing. I am always so proud each June at the former football player golf outing, always hosted by our head coach, obviously, this year, Urban Meyer. Many of you have heard me say "Buckeyes for Life" as well as "The Brotherhood" and it sure rings true each June. Many believe John Cooper was not a "good fit" and was not well liked when he was head coach of the Buckeyes, but each year, he is welcomed back to our outing with open arms. **"Buckeyes for Life"**.

While Earle Bruce always made an appearance at this outing as well, the one that underlines the camaraderie and incredible brotherhood of Varsity "O" Football to me is Gary Moeller. Moeller was captain of TOSU 1965 team, but then went on to a great coaching career at "that school up north,'" the University of Michigan, as well as a stint at the University of Illinois. Regardless, he is welcomed back each year and the Varsity "O" wouldn't have it any other way.

I will never forget being recruited by Moeller while he was at Illinois and everyone had thought I was a lock to accept a scholarship and play for the Illini as my older brother had been captain of the 1975 team, All Big Ten and most valuable player. When I decided to go to Ohio State, my brother said, "I'll root for you in every game you play, except for one." I received letters, calls, and was on the receiving end of many boos and jeers when we played in Champaign in 1979. Moeller received criticism when I passed on Illinois as well.

Moeller left Illinois after three years and went back to Michigan as defensive coordinator from 1980 to 1989 and then was head coach from 1990 to 1994. When I spoke to Moeller, he told me that he too received some of those criticisms. "Quite frankly, it was mostly from the fans," Moeller said. My past teammates at Ohio State gave me some teasing, but it was all good natured. You have to understand that the Ohio State/Michigan rivalry is the most incredible rivalry in Sports. "There was some criticism, but I have always looked back on my days at Ohio State as the best in my life," he said. Once a Buckeye, always a Buckeye." **"Buckeyes for Life"**

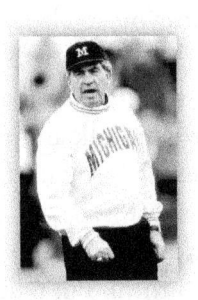

## GARY MOELLER

- Ohio State Football 1961 – 1963
- Ohio State Football Team Captain – 1963
- University of Illinois Head Coach – 1977-1979
- University of Michigan Defensive Coordinator – 1980-1989
- University of Michigan Head Coach – 1990-1994

# TOM LEVENICK

*Archie Griffin shares his thoughts on the bond between former Buckeye football players.*

"To put it in a nutshell, I would say the experiences that we've all shared, some of the experience that we've all had playing for Ohio State, and being a part of great victories and great championships create that "Buckeye Brotherhood." The experience of playing football, playing in Ohio Stadium, playing amongst the hundreds of thousands of fans that come and watch the Buckeyes and shed that Buckeye spirit. It just brings you all close together. It's very, very special. We've all pretty much gone through the same thing. When you play football, you have good times, you have tough times, you have hurts, you have pain, but you all go through those things together and you know that teammate of yours is there with you regardless of what you are going through, you know that that person is going to be—that those guys are going to be on your side. They are a part of your team. They are part of what we accomplish. We accomplish things together and that just makes you so close. So, when you want to be a part of it, you want to continue being a part of it. The good part of it all is that we shared a lot of success together and I don't care what team you talk about, but multiple Ohio State teams when it comes to football that have shared a lot of successes together, and those types of things bring you together and make you want to do things with and be with each other.

"I think I'm talking about differences of what it's like now from being at Ohio State. You take it for granted when you're there in the brotherhood and kind of how much everybody cares about winning each other. Because when you get to the NFL—I'm feeling it a lot more this year, but last year there was a lot of people who didn't really care about you or anybody else but themselves or how much money they're going to make.

"Yes, you take it for granted how good you have it at Ohio State and how great the coaches are. Just the relationships and the brotherhood that's built working together and what else? A big, big switch from going to a place like Ohio State to the NFL. Biggest success was still what you do and what you make of your time off in the off season at Ohio State there really is no off season.

"You're in class year-round and you're at workout, it's mandatory throughout the whole year. You really—you got to be self-reliant and you got to depend on what you—all your work and everything you do for yourself because you don't have somebody like Coach Mick and Coach Meyer in your ear every step of the way telling you what you need to be doing. I think them preparing you like that really, really helped me, and I think I know exactly what I need to do to get where I want to be now."

## Keith Byars gives his thoughts on being a "Buckeye for Life:"

"Before I even got to Ohio State—and talk about growing up in Ohio, watching the Buckeyes every Saturday in the fall, and what it means to be a Buckeye. Just always—especially during the '70s, watching them every New Year's Day in the Rose Bowl. Just watching the camaraderie of the team, especially watching the players in the huddle, hold hands, on offense and defense.

"You knew it's a stronger bond that you always wanted to be a part of. You knew what to do, what exactly it was. As I got older, during my recruiting process, I had the opportunity to talk to many Buckeyes. The person that really stood out the most to me, was Archie Griffin who was playing for the Cincinnati Bengals. We went out and ate lunch together at the Bengals training camp. I sat there and talked to him over lunch, and he was talking about some of the great things about being a Buckeye. He's like, 'I know you're young, but if you come to Ohio State, it will be a part of you for the rest of your life.'

"And all the great players and greatness began in Ohio and Ohio State—you wanted to be a part of it. Ohio State had great players before I came here, and they had great players after I left," Byars said. "You just want to be a part of that great legacy of Ohio State University, Ohio State football, and everything about it." I've always been a historian. I've always loved history, and that was something that really stood out to me. I wanted to be linked in that great chain of strong bond and brotherhood that Ohio State football was about.

"Another person was Woody Hayes. When I talked to Woody Hayes when I was getting recruited, and even during the four years of being at Ohio State, Woody Hayes is the greatest coach to ever coach at Ohio State. Even though I didn't play for him, this conversations that I had with him over the course of the years that I knew him, I always felt like it was a coach-player relationship. I'm like, 'You just drop your pearls of wisdom to me on the field or off the field for the rest of my life.' Once I got to Ohio State to see, all these things that predated me and the conversations I've had before I joined, I knew they were all true. It wasn't just recruiting talk, and it wasn't just rhetoric. And the teammates that I met there, and the bond that you had. You know it's been over 30 years since I've left Ohio State, but once we see each other, it's like we're the same guys. We laugh and joke around. It's the bond that we have together and all the times. You know when we see each other, no matter where we are, whether we're in Columbus or California, it doesn't matter. Whenever we see each other, we know what it's about, what the meaning is of being a Buckeye and the bond that we share with each other.

"My college roommate is still my best friend today, Pepper Johnson. It's like we're brothers, we just have different parents, but we're brothers. I mean when we get on the phone, our wives know to look out. 'They're going to be on the phone for about three hours.'

"You know and we may not have talked in a month or two, but when we talk, we're going to talk like we've just seen each other yesterday. And that's just something when we bond. We just get caught up with each other, and we genuinely care for each other. And whenever someone needs us, we're just a phone call away. Like Mike Tomczak decided to get on the phone and call me and said, 'I need you now on this day, we got four, five, or six guys who just came in from out of town,' we'll be there for each other. That's what we share.

"No, we're nothing like a cult or anything like that, but it's just a strong bond that only comes through blood, sweat, and tears that we've experienced with each other. And when I was living in Florida, I would talk to people about it. You don't know what it's like until you get there. So, the people who grow up in Ohio and go to Ohio State, they get it right away. But the out of towners, the people from Florida, Missouri, California—once they come and they're like, 'Man, this is different.' There's a difference. And once you experience it, it's a difference, means it's a very positive—it's a special bond. They will always be with you no matter where you are.

"Those fervent bonds that brings us all together, once you join the Buckeyes. So, no matter the sport, no matter the competition. I don't care if it's golf, I don't care if it's medicine, mathematics, we want to always be the leaders in that community, and that's something that always links us together. No other university has that, no matter where the sport, no matter where's the bond, that's the bond of Ohio State. That's why we have the largest alumni group. That's why Ohio State when they go to the bowl games, every city wants to get them because they know alumni, they know Ohio State travels not just well, but they travel great to bowl games.

"Because people inside, they have Buckeyes there, whether they're a Bowl in Jacksonville, Florida, or California, Arizona, Texas, there's a Buckeye contingency there waiting to welcome and to welcome people that they know. They support you no matter what you do at Ohio State and your career takes you in different directions around the world, Ohio State connects you to it. When I was in college, I played in the Japan Bowl for the All-Star game. Lo and behold, I ran into an Ohio State alumnus there. He showed us around Tokyo, Japan, when we got over there, me and my teammates. I'm like, 'You guys, we need to look out for Ohio State people.' I'm like, 'I'm in Tokyo, Japan, and I have someone there that's taking me and showing me around Tokyo where to get something to eat.' That was like, wow."

**Teresa Fightmaster has a great perspective on the "Buckeye Sisterhood" or The Ohio State "Swimmin Women"**

"Well, it seems like, even though we don't talk every day, we might shoot emails. Once we get together for reunions, it's like we haven't skipped a beat," Fightmaster said. "I think that bond and the love that we have and all those years we swam together for Jim and Bev, it's something that we're all really proud of, to represent Ohio State. I think every year that you get older, you look back and you realize that you were part of something really special. It had its ups and downs, but we stuck together in those years. We were a part of five Big Ten Championships in a row. Ohio State hasn't done that since, and so we feel like we're pretty special."

Teresa has developed Junior National qualifiers, Sectional qualifiers, Grand Prix qualifiers, YMCA National Runner-up champion and qualifiers, Ohio High School State champions and qualifiers, Quad qualifiers, Zone and Age Group individual and relay champions and qualifiers, placed swimmers in the Top 16 in the Country and had Age Group Individuals as well as Team Hi Point winners. She was the Ohio Age Group Coach of the Year for the 2006-2007 seasons and has served two times as an Ohio Zone coach. She has also served as the Ohio Swimming Age Group rep for Central Ohio and on the

Ohio Swimming Review Board. *"Something tells me that Teresa is a "Bob Fenton" to many of her swimmers."*

**Clark Kellogg, former Buckeye Great Basketball Player adds his thoughts on "Buckeyes for Life" and the Buckeye Brotherhood:"**

I agree that the bond of Ohio State athletes is truly incredible. I think it's beyond just the basketball or the athletics side of it, though. I think there's esprit de corps, a pride, a spirit that is Buckeye nation. I think we have over 550,000 living alumni all over the world, I think, at last count. I don't know if that makes us the largest, but it certainly puts us on the shortlist of living alumni in terms of numbers. There's a tremendous bond between those that are part of the Buckeye family, and certainly, I think it's exacerbated and then magnified a bit in the world of athletics just because of the nature of sports.

"But I think there's a real pride at being an Ohio State grad, being part of that fraternity or alumni base of Buckeyes because of what the state university means. Not just to the people, the state, but to people in the region, and throughout the country, and even in the world now. I think it permeates all aspects of being a Buckeye in the world of sports. Again, the fraternity is special in and of itself when you share the heartache, and the sweat, and the tears, and the bond sports create, and then factor in the prominence of Ohio State as a university, as a difference-maker in society, in the world.

"I think it may go back to the strong Midwest values and a real basic sense of pride. But it is special. I can't go anywhere. Obviously, I'm visible because of what I do and also being 6'9" and black, having played basketball. But I encounter Buckeye fans, fanatics, friends, everywhere. Some of them are not even Buckeye grads [laughs], some of them are just enamored with and appreciative of what Ohio State represents. Yes, I do think it's unique, that sense of pride around one being a Buckeye."

***Tom Skladany had a brief but poignant opinion on why former Buckeye players are so "close knit:"***

"I believe it is because of the way we were taught from Woody and then it was passed down as to how to treat people and your teammates...The one thing Woody always told us was 'Look around the room gentlemen! These guys that you are staring at will be your friends for life."

***That leads me to the third part of this story, which involves Mike Boren. Boren played linebacker for Michigan from 1980 to 1983 and, he also played for Gary Moeller. We are all aware that Mike's son Justin, left the Wolverine program in 2007 to transfer to THE OHIO STATE UNIVERSITY and Mike had two other sons, Zach and Jacoby, subsequently play for the Buckeyes.***

***I always wondered what it must be like being a former "Michigander," having three sons play for your most heated rival. While speaking with Mike, he said what most good fathers would say, but also had some additional thoughts to share.***

"I just want the best for my boys," Boren said. It was pretty tough when Justin decided to leave Michigan for Ohio State, but the Buckeyes welcomed him with open arms. Ohio State has a terrific program and they really take care of their own," he said.

Boren hasn't enjoyed quite the same support at Michigan that Gary Moeller or John Cooper have at Ohio State. "I think most Michigan fans would want to light me on fire," Mike said. Justin and I went to the 2011 Ohio State/Michigan Game in Ann Arbor and it wasn't pretty."

Michigan does not have the number or quality of opportunities for former players as Ohio State does, according to Boren. Boren simply wants his sons to have the best college

football experience and college education possible. "With everything that has happened and the way my boys have been treated at Ohio State, I probably feel more like a Buckeye than I do a Wolverine", he said. "I will always be a former Michigan player and I want Michigan to win every game......., but one. I just want the best for my sons and they had it at Ohio State".
*I like how you put it Tom, "Buckeyes for Life."*

Mike Boren

Mike, Zach and Justin Boren

Prior to his passing, October 29, 2016, I had the pleasure to visit with one of the greatest offensive linemen ever to play college football, John Hicks. As we constantly scrutinize the greatest Buckeyes of all time by position, it can be argued that John Hicks was the greatest Buckeye offensive lineman of all time.

Please review his accomplishments at the end of this section.

Obviously, Hicks was one of the very greatest and no one can surpass his credentials, from any school.

As with many former Buckeye stars, I had the opportunity to visit with John and discuss the changes that he has seen take place in college football from his playing days in the 1970s until today in 2012.

The increased size and speed of players today has been identified by every former player that I have spoken with and

Hicks pointed it out as well. "We didn't have any 300 pond linemen when I played," Hicks said. "Those guys are much bigger. I don't think they are better athletes, but they are a lot bigger than we were," he said

John also pointed out the style of play of the current college football offensive lineman. "Guys today are taught to lead with their hands and use their arms so much more. They don't put their head in the middle anymore," he said. "It is all about position blocking, zone blocking, and protecting the gap. They take a lot more precautions today in keeping guys healthy than they did when we played.

**Archie Griffin spoke recently about the dominance of the Ohio State Offensive lines during Hicks' era by** saying, "They were so good, that we used to come to the line of scrimmage and say, 'we're running here, try to stop it.'"

When I mentioned that statement to Hicks and asked him to comment on it he had a different version. "We used to just tell the little shit not to fumble the ball. Then, we would come to the line of scrimmage and tell the defense, number 45 is going to get the ball, try and stop him. Archie would stick it in the end zone and then come back to us and say would you guys cut that out!," Hicks said laughing

The Ohio State Football and Varsity "O" experience is another aspect that has surfaced during my discussions with each of these former players.

When I asked John, to name his greatest moment in all of football, he didn't hesitate when he replied, "It was the day I was recruited at Ohio State, without a doubt. When I was recruited in February of 1969, I had the opportunity to meet Tim Fox, Kurt Schumacher, Tim Anderson, John Brockington, and Jack Tatum. They were guys who not only became teammates, but became lifelong friends.

John Hicks had a terrific career at Ohio State and in the NFL, with multiple honors, awards, championships and bowl games. It truly amazes me that given all of his accomplishments and experiences his most vivid memory is about establishing that teamwork and lifelong friendships.

I once had the opportunity to experience the intensity of those teammate and lifelong relationships. Ohio State Varsity "O" holds a golf outing each June for the former Varsity "O" football players. It is hosted by the head coach. I will never forget during the awards presentation after our 2009 outing, John Hicks stood up in front of the entire group of former players and implored them to reach out and extend help to one of the greatest Buckeye football players of all time, Jack Tatum. Tatum had suffered from intense diabetes for years and now needed to have his leg amputated from the knee down, but he did not have the insurance or finances to support that extensive surgery.

Hicks made two statements while he solicited help for Tatum. He said, "Once a Buckeye always a Buckeye and 'One Buckeye Down, all Buckeyes down.'" John asked everyone to leave some cash for Jack's surgery on the table in front of him and by the time we left, cash was piled one foot high. Funds were raised for Tatum and he spent another year of comfort, prior to his death in 2010. *"Buckeyes for Life."*

The relationships, the teamwork, the camaraderie and the lifelong bonding elements of Buckeye football and Varsity "O", just like John Hicks demonstrated, do not exist anywhere else in America. Given those elements, I am confident that those lifelong team mates and friendships are an underlying factor in helping Ohio State win consistently and stay at the top year after year. That passion and those elements will endure, right along with Ohio State being at the pinnacle of college football.

Hicks and Woody after beating Michigan in 1974 to earn a trip to the Rose Bowl.

Hicks enshrined into the Rose Bowl Hall of Fame.

## John Hicks

- 1972 All Big Ten
- 1972 All American
- 1973 All Big Ten
- 1973 All American
- 1973 2$^{nd}$ in the voting for the Heisman Trophy
- 1973 Lombardi Trophy
- 1973 Outland Trophy
- 1974 NFC Rookie of the year
- 2009 Rose Bowl Hall of Fame
- Overall Buckeye Record – 28-3-1

***Garth Cox, former buckeye Offensive Tackle talks about the Buckeye Culture:***

"Well, as far as the culture is concerned, I don't know how you feel, but it's an interesting thing. I think the culture becomes stronger the older you get. When you first get out of Ohio State, I mean obviously you're proud to be a Buckeye and all that, but you're focused on so many other things and it's great to see your buddies, but you don't really realize the things that you just said that keep us all together. The ties that bind kind of idea. As you get older, you realize how strong those are, because we do get busy with families. We get busy with jobs, et cetera. But then you get the call from the buddy that either has got a problem or having issues, or has got a great event in their lives, a wedding of a child, or the birth of a grandchild, or something like that. We're all immediately right there for each other. I think as we get older, maybe the culture isn't stronger but the realization of the culture becomes stronger. At least it has with me.

"I think the reason that is, is because, I've never been in the service, but I've always equated it to that whole foxhole mentality that brings servicemen together. I mean you hear guys that fought together, that were in the service, whatever. It's like that old thing, that steel is tempered by fire, and I think it's the same thing. All of us went through a lot of stuff. While I'm not equating it to war or something like that. It was stuff that only we went through and only guys that played at Ohio State went through it. That's at the basis of the culture. That's the good and the bad that we went through. Two days and the coaches and all that, that's 'the bad.' I don't know about your group of guys, but we sit around and bullshit, all of us. We don't really talk about dreams, we talk about junk that happened at practices, or in the Woody Hayes Facility or in the dorms and stuff. Nobody really sits around and says, hey remember that one game we did this.

"To me, the culture is more just all the time we spent together. The things we did and then the things, all the fun we got out of it that we change. To me, that's the culture of Ohio State. It's the bond and the friendship that we built because of the things we went through together. Not just games, and not just practices, but everything. Because it sounds corny but all of us came from being boys to really men during that period of time together. While at least with me and my life, I've always said, there's three people that matter the most to me, it's my dad, my grandpa Litz and Coach Hayes. I've always also said that all of them become smarter, the older I get. Whenever

I give a speech, I always say that, that those three guys, the older I get, the smarter they get. Because stuff when you're teenagers, you don't recognize what they're telling you makes sense and that it's true.

"But the other people that are important are the guys on my team and the Buckeyes. Because we did, we went from 18 to 22 during those four years together. That's a big life-changing experience for a lot of us, and we all did it together. Those are the kinds of things that I think that, at least in my group of guys, we'd look back on, not the games necessarily. We do talk about some games, so for the most part, it's just all the other stuff that's one with being a Buckeye.

"I said that that is a call to the Buckeyes together, because admittedly, the Buckeyes today are a different breed than what we were back when we were there. We didn't have all these camps, we didn't have all these four-star ratings and before you ever put on your uniform, you're the greatest thing since sliced bread and all that which these kids have today. But on the other hand, we did have the stigma of being an Ohio State football player, and that was a very good stigma.

"You and I both know that given today at the age of 62, when somebody finds out I played football in Ohio State, it immediately opens the door. People want to talk to you, they want to ask you about it. Just this past weekend, my son and I were playing together in a golf tournament and the two guys we were playing with, they were about my son's age, 32 to 35 probably.

"One of them was a banker from New York City, an investment banker, and he said, 'Hey, somebody told me you played at Ohio State.' I said, 'Yes. A long time ago.' And all he wanted to do is talk about Ohio State. I wanted to talk about investment banking and what's on the horizon for the economy and all that. But he wants to talk about Ohio State football and hear about Ohio State. I'm sure your experiences are the same.

"It continues, no matter when you played or what your level of play, whether you're a starter or second team or whatever, it opens the doors in conversation for you that you might not otherwise have. Ohio State has done that for me and it has done that for all of us, I think. That's kind of a relevant thing, but I think that's our culture. The culture is that we went through something together. We identified having gone through it together, and as a result, it's clear that this period in our life, no matter what age you are, that you can rely on your Buckeye teammates. That when you're having issues or a trouble or two, they'll always be there for you. I think that's the culture of Ohio State." ***Buckeyes for Life!***

## Garth Cox

- Ohio State Football 1974 – 1977
- 2 Year Letter winner – Left Offensive Tackle
- President of the Varsity "O" Alumni Association – 2014-2016

**Pepe Pearson discusses his views on the "Buckeye Brotherhood:"**

"I backed up Eddie George for two years and then I started, but just recently, you know I'm in the coaching profession and it's great to be able to reach out to a former teammate like Eddie George and ask him to call a current player that I am coaching and talk with him about work ethic and the mentality you need to compete at the highest level. That's what the brotherhood is all about, because he knows I wouldn't be calling him unless the person I want him to help is that important and needs that from him and he knows I would do that for him as well." ***Buckeyes for Life!***

### Pepper Johnson talks about being a "Buckeye for Life:"

"I lived by myself. I think everybody goes out of their way to reach out. We have had some players that have had some tough times. A lot of us were at the hospital when Dave passed away. Everybody gets the word around and everybody is about the guys are doing the right thing and taking trips and trying to be there.

"Everybody is doing this from their heart. It's not a publicity stunt. We care about it, no one is broadcasting it or advertising it, I think the word that we were there got out. Other than that, everybody was doing this from their heart. I have some teammates that were from Virginia, Florida, and California. All they talked about was giving it all."

### Buckeye Women's Basketball Hall of Famer Katie Smith is a "Buckeye for Life and feels the "Buckeye Sisterhood."

"We have a 'Buckeye Sisterhood' that is great," Smith said. "You saw a few of them come back for the '93 team reunion. As you know, as we get older and life happens, it's hard to coordinate a day or a weekend. Whether you talk on a consistent basis, or you just reach out after months of not talking or even a year, it's like no time has really passed. It's a lot of fun to have that. People you run into, whether it's folks that are working in college basketball or still in the basketball world. Or those that are just around town, you see their kids or you see posts on Facebook or you reach out and say, "Hey, you want to come to this?" All those relationships are there whether they're a weekly, monthly, they're just somebody who you always feel comfortable with having a conversation and catching up. That connection just never dies."

**Current Buckeye Defensive End and 2017 Big Ten Defensive Lineman of the Year, Nick Bosa is a "Buckeye for Life" and truly embraces the "Buckeye Brotherhood."**

"We definitely appreciate the brotherhood and I felt that last year, but this year I really felt it," Bosa said. "Just the older guys bringing the younger guys along. There just really isn't a person on our team that I can't go up to and give a hug and feel completely normal about. Everybody's good buddies on the team and it's not just like a job. It's more of a passion. It's what we love to do and we all do it together and we love each other. That's what the brotherhood is to me."

***Doug Plank shares his views on the Ohio State culture:***

"Here is what I think. Number one, I think if there is a tremendous amount, if you just level the playing field right now, would it take time for Ohio State to establish itself? Yes, it would. But it's the people that have been there before, I don't even know how to explain it. It's like you're recruiting athletes and trying to get out there and do the job. But somewhere, somehow down there below the surface this university, this coaching staff across a lot of different sports have done an incredible job of finding those people that life matters to them. They are not just people who are trying to go out there and try to get a scholarship, go play somewhere, go try to move on to the next level and make money, whatever.

"There is something about the quality of the athletes they have been able to draft—but not draft, to recruit, and have within their organization that makes them what they are. I didn't make Ohio State, I didn't even add one little teeny little smidgen to it, it was already there when I got there. I never ever thought about Ohio State even being an option for me in high school because it was up the stratosphere [laughs]. They had just won a national championship a couple of years earlier, that was the closest thing you could get to the ability of the pros. Their program spoke for itself, and that's why when the opportunity came—everything in life you can say, 'You have got to take advantage of all your opportunities and blah blah.'

"You know what though, Tom? Those certain opportunities come within a very small window and if you don't take it at that time, it's gone. It's like you're going to the shopping market, you are going to the grocery and they keep changing their stock all the time, they don't have the same bananas or fruits or choices that they have every week, it's almost like Costco or something. You go there, if you don't take advantage of this at this time, it's going to be gone for the rest of your life, and it's flashing right in front of you. That's the same as with Ohio State, when you hear them say you're going win a championship, so accept a scholarship to come to Ohio State, that was it.

"It wasn't any more difficult than that. I know there were some stories out there, that I'd been sending letters to Joe Paterno and all that sort of thing. Joe Paterno, they had a great program at Penn State too, but they were winning a lot of games. But it wasn't like Ohio State, and sometimes when you grow up and you're a young kid, you're scared of going any place. I've only been outside the state of Pennsylvania twice in my whole life as a senior in high school. So, the safe choice was to go to Penn State. That was where everybody else went that lived in the area.

"But I think it's a job that Ohio State can do in terms of attracting, not only kids that are talented, but the right kids, for the tradition. There was an event out here in Arizona where it was at one of the games down here and Ohio State was playing. I had a chance to meet some of the other athletes who had played in different sports for Ohio State over the years.

"I was just talking to them; one girl in particular was on the OSU Women's swim team from Illinois. I asked her, I said, 'What in the world made you choose Ohio State over another school?' I said, 'What was it?' She said, 'I came to a football game.' She said, 'I've never seen anything like that in my life.' She said, 'That made my decision.' I said, 'So you came to a football game to make a decision, you then go to Ohio State to swim?' She goes, 'Yes. I can't explain it. I couldn't explain it to my parents. Way back in the day, I'm just telling you, Doug, today, here, right now. That's what it was. That's what made the difference.'

"I've never ever heard anybody ever say anything like that from a cross sports standpoint, Yes, I went to play football there because they had a great baseball team or a great basketball team,' and she said, 'That was just the people that were there. The support, I've never seen anything like it.' I try to explain sometimes when I go to other schools and other places. You always want to be respectful of all schools, their alumni, and all that sort of thing. I just say, 'You don't need to say anything about the event. It speaks for itself.'

"The first game, we grew up in Pennsylvania; Western Pennsylvania, just outside of Pittsburgh, we're huge Pitt fans, Steeler fans, Penn State fans. My mother comes in the first game and just sits in the stands. Afterwards, she still had tears in her eyes.

"We won the game, it was not anything, we were expected to win. We did win 56 to -0- or something. She goes, 'Doug, I'm just still trying to get a hold of myself,' and I said, 'Why?' She goes, 'I have never seen anything like the band coming on the field like that.' And she said, 'I just started crying uncontrollably.' [laughs] I went, 'What?' She was, 'Yes, I just couldn't control myself, I don't know what it was.'

"But I think you add up all those things, Tom, and on top of it, it's great tradition of the school and all of the other factors. I just think it's not a normal course of what you would expect out of life and we maybe have become too accustomed to going other places where they have good teams and great things happen and all that sort of thing. But, I don't know, there's just something about Ohio State, the tradition, the players. To me—I don't know, when I came in they didn't have the greatest facilities at that time. Obviously, The Woody Hayes Center or whatever wasn't built yet. We had the Ernie Biggs North Athletic Facility which was pretty conservative versus the W.H.A.C. You learn very quickly that this place is special and the people that are there are very special and it's not about you, it's about Ohio State and you will be spending four years of your life coming through there at the same time though—hopefully, you can add to it in some small part, some small way that maybe you left a little footprint there. This had a huge impact on my life, it really did, it gave me direction and the guys that have come out of there were so successful."

**Ernie Andria has some great thoughts about or Buckeye Bond:**

"You know me; I'm a glass half-full guy all the time. I'm such a positive guy and I have so many memories. Woody always talked to us about that, our bond, all the time. He beat it into our heads about how we're going to have these memories to share this bond for the rest of our lives, no matter where we're at, all over the country. That's all you heard, and everything that he said was all so true. And now that we're 60 years old and approaching, Lev and we all stay in close touch and help each other. you know what I mean?" *"Buckeyes for Life!"*

**Cornelius Green shares more thoughts on the Buckeye Brotherhood:**

"Meeting so many younger players who embrace the older guys like myself really makes you feel good, man. So, I'm glad we finally had a chance to have this conversation, reminisce about how great our years were at Ohio State, in addition to a lifelong time of great friends. For me, my freshman year class is coming up for my 45th year reunion and I can't wait to see these guys as we have stayed in touch and I remember these guys vividly." *"Buckeyes for Life!"*

**Eric Kumerow also expresses his thoughts on the "Buckeye Brotherhood:"**

"One of our fellow teammates was battling some demons here not too long ago. He was in bad shape. He was in really bad shape. Four or five of us rallied the troops together and we took a road trip and we went to go see him, and he was in bad shape. I think the fact that he saw his brothers just standing there looking at him, I think it had a big impact on him coming back from where he was. You know what I mean? When you're talking about your situation with your surgery and waking up and seeing your boys standing there, that's pretty much what we did for him and he's doing great, just great.

"All the victories, all the championships, all the bowl wins and all the stuff, you're reveling in those victories together as a team, and you're also shedding blood, sweat, tears, broken bones, everything else together. It's almost like being in a foxhole, and you bond for life," Kumerow said.

"There's a certain brotherhood that forms when you're making a commitment to play a game like college football, especially at Ohio State. The big games, the tough losses, the big wins. I mean, it's just a part of your life that should never be replaced no matter what you go on and do. You can't replace that.

"The five short years that I spent on campus in Columbus, Ohio, I made not tons and tons of friends, but deep, deep down inside there's probably five or six guys that are my friends for life to this day. They all stood up in my wedding. I stood up in all their weddings. We may not talk every day and the time does slip away trying to get by a little bit, but I guarantee If we needed each other, there's no doubt that any one of us would be there for each other." **"Buckeyes for Life"**

## Maurice Hall is firmly a part of the "Buckeye Brotherhood:"

"I think it comes down to a few things. One I think is the tradition. Growing up in Columbus and being able to see Ohio State Football from the outside of the institution, one thing that stuck out to me was the tradition of the Ohio State team whether it was, like you said, internal pride or maybe even the getting recruited and going out there to see them do their thing, visiting the facilities, and watch them practicing. Everyone has the same mindset of excellence and wanting to be the best team. Because of that, I think it holds the team together.

"The Championship ethic at Ohio State, that's what stuck out to me, is everyone just wanting to be the best. And because everyone wanted to be the best and having that common bond, that was the reason why we won the national championship in 2002. We then just continue to move forward and the great teams we've had since then, it's the tradition. And the people that we bring to Ohio State I think are unique people. We recruit, to a certain extent, a certain kind of player, a certain kind of person. I think that the people we bring, they all have this similar background aspect of just wanting to be great, but also wanting to be a good person and because of that, I think that's who we are." **"Buckeyes for Life"**

***Stanley Jackson, has some great perspective on our "Buckeye Brotherhood:"***

"You know how it is, when you're here, it's your kingdom. It's your castle. When you're playing, you really aren't connected to the people that came before you, and you don't even have a thought about anybody coming after you. It's your number. It's your town. It's your school. You take ownership, and it's personal. Then you transition, and I call them dinosaurs. You end up being one of these dinosaurs walking around that people are captivated by still to this day," Jackson said.

"But the thing that stands out to me the most is even though I recognized the player because he played 30 years before me or five years or ten years after me, when you meet former players, there's an instant connection. The history ties us all together. We've all played for different head coaches. All their philosophies and how they run things is different, but they all value the legacy of Ohio State Football and cherish all their players and former players. As a player, once you're done playing at Ohio State, to me that connection is second to none.

"I've been around guys who played at other places, and like you said earlier, it's just not the same. My gut tells me, maybe it's all the tradition and all the history that ties it together, but there's a real family. There's a real camaraderie. I met Cornelius Greene for the first time a few years ago, in person, and it was like we've known each other 20 years. The way we embraced each other, it was significant.

"When I see these quarterbacks coming out like when Kenny Guiton was in transition. It was like, 'What can I do to help you go to the next level?' That to me is sensational. I don't know if there's a lot of places like that around the country where we are brothers in arms. Whether you played for Woody, Earl, John Cooper, Jim Tressel, or Urban Meyer,

when you're done, there's this connection that's significant."
***"Buckeyes for Life"***

**Matt Finkes share his thoughts on the "Buckeye Brotherhood" and being a "Buckeye for Life:"**

"It's funny—I think that it's tough to put a finger on what makes that relationship so special. I've talked to a lot of different guys. Playing in the NFL, you talk to a lot of different guys from different schools and when you describe to them what it's like to be a Buckeye, they can't grasp it. Even now, when I go back and do some stuff or there are friends who come in town and you're doing the charity golf outings or fundraisers and stuff like that or just if you need something from someone, you can pick up the phone and call them, it's tough to put a finger on it.

"I think that it's just the culture, I think it's the culture of, maybe, even the university as a whole, not just as the football team. I think that it has filtered down, it's more condensed and it's more tangible and real at the football level, but at the university, as a whole, the alumni association and just the community—and I've got the opportunity to speak to a lot of different alumni association gatherings over the past three, four years all over the country, anywhere from Phoenix to Orlando. I was just down in Charleston, South Carolina, and a couple of weeks ago, in Atlanta.

"You have these pockets of Ohio State people and they're everywhere, they're so passionate about what their school represents and I think it's that passion, filtered down through the lens of going through what you go through in football, and then that being, basically, your family, maybe not even your second family, but your first family, I mean you see them more than your first family for the four years [laughs] when you're here playing. So, I think there's that real sense of family that goes along with that and again, I think it's just the culture.

"I think it's the culture that the university breeds and then I think it's the culture that comes down from Woody Hayes, to Earl, to Tressel, and to Urban. The brotherhood is a word that we used back in the '90s and brotherhood is a word that Urban uses today.

"I'm sure brotherhood was a word the Woody used and Earl used. I think that, again, ingraining of the culture of, "These are guys that you're going to do anything for and they're going to do anything for you'.' And that mentality, maybe it goes back to Woody having that military mentality with this football team and it carrying forward all the way to Urban Meyer. But, I think that there's more to it than just what the football and athletics teams are. I think that at a grander level—I tell the story, all the time, about I was playing at NFL Europe and I had an Ohio State sweat-shirt or t-shirt on and we were going through the Berlin airport. I had a guy come up to me and say, 'OH', and I said, 'IO' to him.

"I bet the guys on the team, that they asked me what it was about and I told them. I said, 'I will bet you $100, I could stand here in the middle of the Berlin airport and I'll yell, 'OH' and someone else will yell, 'I-O.'" I won the bet [laughter] because there's Ohio State people everywhere. I think it's, again, that culture; it's the pride of the state, it's the pride of the school, and then it filters down into a more condensed level with the guys that you spend four or five years with, sweating and going through hell, and picking each other up and being there through, not just hard times in football, but hard times in life.

"I think that that's just ingrained in us. Whether it was through the coaching staff or through the people, I think, again, that word, brotherhood, has been used for the 20 plus years that I've been associated with the OSU football program. That's gone across three different coaches, four if you count Luke. That's something that, I think, coaches understand here and it's something that's probably taught to them and passed down and they ingrain it in the players."

**Tim Burke has a moving story about being a Buckeye for Life:**

"It's 1979 and Bill Jaco and I are competing to be the starting tackles for the 79 season. As I recall, it was me, you- Tom, Jake, Joe Lukens, and "Bear" Brown (Tim). We go out for warm up for the first game of the year, which was Syracuse, right?

"Okay. We go out for a warm up and we come back in. We're milling around the locker room and Coach Myles says, 'Jaco, Burke, follow me.' Okay, then he takes us somewhere, I don't know where it was. We were not around anybody else. Buddy Myles is looking down and he looks up and he's rubbing his face and he goes, 'I don't know how to say this any other way but I'm going to say it.'

"He said, 'you both have been here four years and you both worked very hard and I know this is the big moment-because I was starting my very first day ever in my life. Jaco had actually started a few other times at tight end. He's played a lot.' Myles said, Jake was playing right tackle and I was playing left tackle. He said, 'You two are going to start this game. After this game, one of you is not going to be starting. Joe Lukens is going to be the other starting tackle because that's just the way it's going to be, he's that good. I'm sorry to tell you this way, but the way that we have decided, we're going to determine who is going to be starting by your performance today and you will start at the tackle spot that Lukens doesn't pick.' It's going to be based on whoever grades out the highest in this game. He said, 'I'm sorry,' and he turned around and walked away. Jake's all upset and he looks at me, he said, 'God damn 'Burkey,' after four fucking years of all the shit we've done, all the things we've been through and it's going to come down to this?' He goes, 'One of us isn't going to be starting next week.' He goes, 'I don't want it to be me,' but he goes, 'I don't want it to be you either.'

"Inside, I was struggling. Because I remembered something Woody said to us. I've used it and thought of it so many times in my life. Because he said, 'nothing in life that comes easy to you is ever worth a damn.'

"It's a community ultimately and I'm sitting there looking at Jake and I wanted Jake to start next week, but I wanted to start too, because all I ever wanted to do was hear the stadium announcer say, 'starting at left tackle for the Buckeyes, number 76, Tim Burke from Wapakoneta, Ohio.' All while my parents are sitting in Ohio stadium one time and hear that, that's all I ever wanted.

"Thirty-eight years later, Bill Jaco says, 'Burkey and I are great friends for life and I will do anything for him.' Tim Burke added, 'There is nothing more intense than the Buckeye Brotherhood and Jake and I will be close friends and brothers for the rest of our lives." ***"Buckeyes for Life"***

**Kirk Herbstreit talks about being a "Buckeye for Life:"**

"Yes, I was the typical kid in the State of Ohio; pre-internet, pre-gadgets. Growing up in the '70s Ohio State era for me, and just a little bit before that, it was literally mythical.

"All the people you talk to, I can assure you not one person who lived Ohio State Football the way I did. I don't mean to say that to challenge anybody, but my friends make fun of me because—forget playing for Ohio State. I knew everything about everything regarding Ohio State Football from the time I can remember. I used to purposely try to not listen to the game and hear the score of the game, then I would watch Paul Warfield on WOSU at ten o'clock at night like the game was live. My parents would let me stay up to watch the game and I would work so hard to stay up and try not to hear the score of the game. Do you know how hard it is to not find out the score of an Ohio State game?

"And then watch Paul Warfield, I can't remember the other guy. They used to call the games. But those used to be such awesome memories. I knew every player's jersey number. It was the most off the charts passion of mine.

"My parents used to say I was just weird, to be seven, eight years old, and I would just sit in front of the TV and when games were on, I would just watch. Not talk, not move, and not—I was just—Again, I don't know how to describe it rather than it was just like the players were mythical, like Zeus or something to me, like superheroes or something.

"My dad played there, obviously, he was captain there. He coached with Woody, he coached with Bo. He used to take me to the locker room when we'd go to games. It wasn't like every game, but once a year, we would go in and see Woody Hayes and I would put on Archie's helmet and it was just surreal. It was very hard to be seven or eight years old and look up at these guys and It would be like if a kid today met Superman, and Superman was real or Batman was real. That's what it was like for me meeting these guys in the locker room and it just stuck with me my whole life.

"As I grew up and I started to play high school football in the state of Ohio and started to have a little bit of success and Earle Bruce was the coach, it started to become a reality that I might be able to be recruited at a pretty high level. I used to go to bed at night and there was time if you remember, the Soviet Union and the United States in the cold wars in the mid-late 80s. It was about nuclear wars and things. I used to go to bed and pray to God that if the world is going to end with nuclear bombs, can you just let me go to Ohio State and please let me play football for the Buckeyes before the end of the earth.

"I am dead serious. It meant everything to me to have a chance to go there. Honestly, I think that's why I really struggled initially the first two or three years. I just couldn't believe that I was in that locker room. I couldn't believe that I was wearing that scarlet and gray jersey.

"It was really hard for me to be like, 'I belong here, I'm good enough to be in here' because I was looking around at people like they were Jim Laughlin, and Todd Bell, and Vince Skillings, and Mike Guess, and Marcus Marek, and Gary Williams, and Doug Donley, and Cal Murray, and Art Schlichter, Archie Griffin. I was just looking around at all these guys like, 'How am I in here? God. How did they let me in here?'

"Anyway, I think that looking back at it, I think it took me a while to calm down and realize, 'Okay, I can do this.' The guys I played with used to tease me because none of them really followed Ohio State. They were great athletes, but they used to kid me about Jack Park. I was like the Jack Park of our team, just because I knew everything about the Buckeyes and the dudes used to just wear me out with my Ohio State knowledge.

"When you come in as a freshman, the coaches hand out a sheet to learn the fight song and all that stuff and I'm like, 'I've known this since I was three, I got it.'

"I think it was just the lessons that I learned at Ohio State. I was an all-world high school recruit like a lot of guys and everybody in the media thought it was a foregone conclusion that I was going to go to Ohio State, start for three or four years, win championships, and all of a sudden, I fell flat on my face. I think I learned so much about getting through tough times.

"There's so many players today I feel so bad for because first sign of adversity, they transfer. For me, my dad probably had as much to do with me learning this as much as anybody because I was ready, when things don't go. When you have all these lofty expectations, I'm like, okay, I'm going to go play baseball, which is another sport I excelled at.

"I'm going to go talk to Bob Todd (Then, Ohio State's baseball Coach) and I'm done with football. It was embarrassing. I didn't want to go back home, people would be like, 'What's going on? Why aren't you playing?' It takes a really strong person to be able to look in the mirror, be honest with yourself and say, 'I'm going to get through this, I need to get better here, I need to get better there,' and dealing a little bit with some politics of the sport. Instead of giving up, I just kept fighting and I really learned about perseverance and work ethic and I had to support my teammates, which was invaluable.

"Behind closed doors my junior year, I was in somewhat of a quarterback controversy, knowing that my guys in that locker room, they had my back, it probably helped me as much as anything to keep pushing and eventually I had to put everything into my senior year, went on to becoming unanimous captain, which the players vote on. It's probably the greatest honor that I had. MVP, got voted again by your teammates, but really winning the captaincy, not only because my dad was a captain, but because of what I'd been through and for my teammates to recognize me, man, you know what? That's our guy. That's our leader. That meant everything to me.

"And then we went out and a couple of my buddies and I were talking about it the other day about how—In fact I was talking to Eddie George about it, just about how great that '92 team could have been. We had some injuries to some of our key players. Like you and everybody else, you can go through each season and say, 'Boy, we could have done this, could have done that, who knows?' But I think it's just the comradery and the love that we had for each other that is probably the thing that I remember the most. Probably like every era, the 70s, 80s, 90s, every group remembers that. My case would be no different."

# EPILOGUE

We as former players have all enjoyed experiences of a lifetime that have made us "Buckeyes for Life." It brings a smile to my face when each and every one of my "Buckeye Brothers" has shared with me that they all have incorporated a Buckeye Element into their funerals or memorial services. Some would like *Across the Field* and *Carmen Ohio* played. Some are planning to have an OSU pep band play. Some have asked for their ashes to be spread in Ohio Stadium and some have asked to be buried, still wearing their championship rings.

Life is a competition. You compete for positions and promotions at work. You compete for the best parking spot. You compete for the best spot in the checkout lane at the grocery store. You compete for the best table at a restaurant. You compete to have the best looking lawn in your neighborhood. On and on and on! There are many life lessons within this book that facilitated The Ohio State Buckeyes being the best competitors and winners possible. These life lessons and characteristics, when applied to everyday life, will foster success and wonderful life fulfillment.

There are so many of these life lessons that we, as former players, learned from the coaching, direction, and examples set by great Buckeye coaches like Woody Hayes, Earle Bruce, Jim Tressel, and Urban Meyer. Those life lessons like "Winning with People," "Paying Forward," the teachings of discipline, making everyone feel appreciated, building confidence, education and development, community involvement, all of which are stressed continuously at Ohio State, have led to great successes after football and off the field for the "Buckeye Brotherhood." The number of former players who have gone on to executive leadership positions in their careers as well as chief legal and political roles and entrepreneurial roles is incredible. We have all benefitted from our experience, education and development at Ohio State.

I have personally benefitted from those lessons that allowed me to be quite successful in leadership roles and provided a great experiential platform to mold, develop, and inspire my employees over the years. I now plan on using this book as a further platform for motivational speaking engagements where I can help others to "Win with People" and to "Pay Forward." ***"Buckeyes for Life" O – H!***

# APPENDIX "A"
# IT'S GREAT TO BE A BUCKEYE

1. It's great to be a Buckeye because you'll never have to be a Wolverine

2. It's great to be a Buckeye because Lebron James considers himself a Buckeye

3. It's great to be a Buckeye because the greatest golfer in History, Jack Nicklaus, is proud to be a Buckeye

4. It's great to be a Buckeye because we have the "Incomparable" Script Ohio.

5. It's great to be a Buckeye because we have the "Best Damned Band in the Land"

6. It's great to be a Buckeye because we have Seven Heisman Trophy winners

7. It's great to be a Buckeye because Mark May <u>is not</u> a Buckeye.

8. It's great to be a Buckeye because Kirk Herbstreit <u>is</u> a Buckeye

9. It's great to be a Buckeye because Bobby Knight is a Buckeye

10. It's great to be a Buckeye because Woody Hayes was the greatest Buckeye ever.

11. It's great to be a Buckeye because Richard Lewis is a Buckeye

12. It's great to be a Buckeye because Bob Hope was a Buckeye

13. It's great to be a Buckeye because Jesse Owens was a Buckeye

14. It's great to be a Buckeye because we have a winning record against Michigan in my lifetime.

    a. 1959 to the Present

15. It's great to be a Buckeye because we have Eight National Titles … and counting

16. It's great to be a Buckeye because of Clark Kellogg

17. It's great to be a Buckeye because you get to "Hang On, Sloopy"

18. It's great to be a Buckeye because you get to hear the Victory Bell on Saturday afternoons.

19. It's great to be a Buckeye because John Glenn was a Buckeye.

20. It's great to be a Buckeye because you get to go to the "Shoe" with 108,000 of your closest friends.

21. It's great to be a Buckeye because you'll always receive a resounding I-O, in exchange for your O-H!

22. O-H, I-O. The code is performed throughout the world. This past October, I was sitting in a small outdoor bar in Rome. The bartender smiled, pointed at me and said, "O, H", to which I responded, "I, O". It happened to a friend

of mine in an OSU shirt at the Eiffel Tower and another friend vacationing in Australia. What do Cornhuskers do?

23. It's great to be a Buckeye because we have had 196 first team All-Americans.

24. It's great to be a Buckeye because we have had five Outland Trophy winners, awarded to the best interior lineman in college football.

25. It's great to be a Buckeye because we have had six Lombardi Trophy winners, more than any other school. The Lombardi is awarded to the best college football lineman or linebacker.

26. It's great to be a Buckeye because we have had a Fred Biletnikoff Trophy winner, awarded to the best receiver in college football.

27. It's great to be a Buckeye because we have had two Jim Thorpe Trophy winners, awarded to the best defensive back in college football.

28. It's great to be a Buckeye because we have had two Dick Butkus Trophy winners, awarded to the best linebacker in college football.

29. It's great to be a Buckeye because we have had four Maxwell Award winners. The Maxwell is given to the best player in college football each year as voted upon by a panel of sports writers and NCAA Head Football Coaches,

30. It's great to be a Buckeye because of Mirror Lake. The Thursday before we beat Michigan, students jump into Mirror Lake to bring the team good luck. This doesn't make a lot of sense, but it is a cool tradition.

31. It's great to be a Buckeye because of Buckeye Grove. Every time a Buckeye player is named a first team All-American, a buckeye tree is planted in Buckeye Grove in their honor.

32. It's great to be a Buckeye because of Gold Pants awarded to the players after beating Michigan.

33. It's great to be a Buckeye because of THE GAME that we get to win every November.

34. It's great to be a Buckeye because of the Senior Tackle

35. It's great to be a Buckeye because of the pecan rolls served to the team the night before Buckeye Games

36. It's great to be a Buckeye because some of the greatest coaches in the history of College Football, all coached for the Buckeyes in their career. Coaches like Woody Hayes, Bo Schembechler, Lou Holtz, Earle Bruce, Glenn Mason, Pete Carrol, Nick Saban, Bill Mallory, Dave McClain, Mark Dantonio

37. It's great to be a Buckeye because of the pre-game skull session in St. John Arena by TBDBITL.

38. It's great to be a Buckeye because we play AC/DC as the team begins warmups.

39. It's great to be a Buckeye because you get to watch Appalachian State beat Michigan.

40. It's great to be a Buckeye because you get to sing *Carmen Ohio* with the team after Buckeye victories.

41. It's great to be a Buckeye because we have more players who have played in the NFL than any other Big Ten team.

42. It's great to be a Buckeye because we award Buckeye Leaves for outstanding plays, to be displayed on the silver helmets. The first helmet sticker awards ever given.

43. It's great to be a Buckeye because of the Tunnel of Pride.

44. It's great to be a Buckeye because we have won 36 Big Ten Championships.

45. It's great to be a Buckeye because we have played in 44 bowl games.

46. It's great to be a Buckeye because of "Real Life Wednesdays".

47. It's great to be a Buckeye because of the Captains Dinner.

48. It's great to be a Buckeye because we are ranked as the #1 team of all time by the Associated Press

49. It's great to be a Buckeye because the Ohio State vs Michigan Game is rated as the Greatest Rivalry in North American Sport by ESPN – ahead of The Red Sox vs Yankees, The Bears vs Packers, Jack Nicklaus vs Arnold Palmer, and Muhammed Ali vs Joe Frasier.

50. It's great to be a Buckeye because the 2015 College Football National Championship between Ohio State and Oregon was the highest viewed sporting event in ESPN history.

# APPENDIX "B"
# HAVE TOM LEVENICK SPEAK TO YOUR GROUP

Tom Levenick

1979 Tackles and Tight Ends

Tom Levenick graduated in Journalism from The Ohio State University in 1984. He is a former Ohio State football player, having played for Woody Hayes and Earle Bruce and in three bowl games – The Gator Bowl, Rose Bowl and Fiesta Bowl. He also was a finisher in the 1989 Hawaiian Ironman Triathlon World Championship. Levenick went on to many Vice

President level leadership positions with companies such as The Winterbrook Beverage Group, Coors Brewing Company, Labatt USA and now, President of PowerPlay Strategies. He has used many of the philosophies and experiences from *"Buckeyes for Life"* as a springboard to success in business. **He can help you do the same.**

*To book Tom for an appearance and motivational speech at your next Alumni Event, Business Meeting or Awards Ceremony, please visit the following websites:*

- http://www.athletepromotions.com/speaker/tom-levenick.php
- https://www.allamericanspeakers.com/speakers/Tom-Levenick/403087
- Sports Speakers 360 – 855-303-5450

# APPENDIX "B" *(continued)*
# HAVE TOM LEVENICK SPEAK TO YOUR GROUP

"I had the honor and privilege to work for Tom Levenick while he was VP of Sales at Coors. Not only was he a great boss I looked up to, he became a very dear friend for life. Tom has a great public speaking presence. He is a true leader and someone that only comes around once in a lifetime. Leaders can choose two very different styles…Lead by Fear or Lead for Inspired Performance. Tom chose the latter and it showed by the high-performance team he created at Coors, coupled with the industry awards we were recognized for. I employ many of Tom's management styles today. The core value Tom cherishes the most is his passion for people; this holds true both on and off the field. I had the privilege to experience the biggest rivalry in college sports at an Ohio State vs. Michigan game in Columbus, seated on the 40-yard line with Tom. That is something I cherish and will never forget."

*John Losasso*
Coors Brewing Co.
1989 – 2013

## TOM LEVENICK

As a non-Buckeye, I found Tom Levenick's book a treat for ALL fans of college athletics. Tom's remarkable skills as a writer, storyteller and a person who lives for the principles of sportsmanship are clearly defined on every page. His skills as a motivational speaker are without peer. Invest a little time with Tom's book and you'll be richly reminded that teamwork, commitment, and character are as much a part of college football as the first chill of Fall and a pigskin.

***Martin Shain***
Business Development Director
Collegiate Sports Fan
Parent to College Athletes
Friend for Life

CPSIA information can be obtained
at www.ICGtesting.com
Printed in the USA
LVHW040921211118
596369LV00001B/1/P

9 781640 852518